A
DONKEY DOCTOR'S
DIARY

Best Wishes

ED Sanderson

A
DONKEY DOCTOR'S
DIARY

Dr Elisabeth D. Svendsen MBE

Whittet Books

Whittet Books Limited, Hill Farm, Stonham Rd, Cotton, Stowmarket, Suffolk IP14 4RQ

British Library Cataloguing in Publication Data
A catalogue record for this book is available from the British Library

The Donkey Sanctuary is at Sidmouth Devon EX10 0NU
Tel (01395) 578222
Fax (01395) 579266
Registered Charity No 264818
Web site: www.thedonkeysanctuary.org

ISBN 1 873580 62 2

Acknowledgments
With special thanks for the photographs to Dan Bryan, Paul Svendsen, June Evers and Bill Tetlow.

The author and publishers are grateful to the following for permission to reproduce photographs that appear on these pages: Miss Maureen Flenley, p. 11; Mr B.R. Jones, St Ives, Cambridge, p. 147; The *Blackpool Gazette*, p. 169; The *Veterinary Record*, p. 193

Printed and bound by Midas Printing International Ltd China on behalf of Compass Press

Dedicated to June Evers, my lifelong friend,
whose wonderful support to me and help with donkey care worldwide has
been of tremendous value.

C O N T E N T S

P R E F A C E

For readers who have not read my previous books – *Down Among the Donkeys* and *For the Love of Donkeys* – here is a brief resumé of what I had been doing up to 1992, when this book starts.

I never meant to care for more than a few donkeys and, in fact, when in 1969 I bought my first donkey, Naughty Face, I had little idea of where my acquisition would lead me.

As a child I had always loved donkeys. Every third weekend, as we visited my grandparents in Lancashire, my father had to make a detour – just so that we could stop at a field where donkeys grazed. I would climb onto the fence and shout 'Donkeys' and they would come running up to me. I trained as a teacher, and obtained a 1st Class Froebel degree, with a particular interest in children with special needs. I married in 1954 and, due to a crisis at my father's company, I resigned as a teacher and became Company Secretary for a pipe works, eventually becoming, I would imagine, the only woman to travel in drain pipes!

My husband's job took us to Somerset and, with one baby and another on the way, nappy drying became a nightmare, as the flat where we were living had no drying facilities. Together my husband and I invented a clothes dryer and we entered a 'Get Ahead' contest on television for the best marketable idea. We won a prize of £5,000 amid massive publicity! We built up the business and were taken over by Thorn Industries, being made Directors of one of their subsidiaries. After two years we resigned to find another challenge, and became business consultants in Cornwall, where we put a shipyard back on its feet amongst other work! Unfortunately my husband injured his back and to find a project we could still do together we bought the Salston Hotel at Ottery St Mary – and I bought 'Naughty Face'. Whilst running the hotel my love and respect for these humble, hard-working animals grew, and I joined the Donkey Breed Society to learn all I could about them. My horror at the condition of donkeys in markets – and one particular incident in Exeter market, where sick, elderly donkeys were sold to a beach operator – made me decide to stop breeding donkeys and start rescuing them.

It was around this time that I first heard from Violet Philpin, who was running the Helping Hand Donkey Sanctuary near Reading. She was deeply devoted to donkeys, but was unable to cope with six donkeys she had rescued from Reading market in very bad condition. I agreed to take them into our care. They were absolutely terrified and in an appalling condition. One little donkey in particular, whom we named Tiny Titch, had obviously been beaten badly, and the solid lumps on his back turned out to be pieces of sacking embedded into his flesh, as well as small broken pieces of bone from his spine. He was so weak that an operation to remove the sacking and remove the splintered pieces of bone had to be postponed until he was stronger. So Shy, another little donkey in this group, was so thin and frightened that it was difficult to get close enough to check her teeth to determine her age. On achieving this, however, I was horrified to find that all her front teeth were broken, with congealed blood still on the gums. She, too, had been severely beaten. An operation to repair her mouth was essential, as she was unable to eat, but she came through it well and was gradually nursed back to health. There is a happy ending to this story; So Shy and Tiny Titch fell in love! When they were both fully recovered they were the first donkeys to go out under our foster scheme, and they spent many happy years together at a foster home not far from the Sanctuary.

The story of how I came to set up The Donkey Sanctuary in Sidmouth, including a legacy of 204 donkeys, is told in my first book, *Down Among the Donkeys*. It also relates how my love of children and background in teaching encouraged me to set up a second charity, The Slade Centre, in 1975, to give children with special needs the opportunity to ride and enjoy close contact with donkeys.

Realising that there were millions of donkeys overseas needing help, particularly working donkeys, I decided, in 1976, to establish a third charity, The International Donkey Protection Trust (IDPT). Today, our teams are helping literally thousands of donkeys every day by providing free veterinary treatment and giving practical advice to the owners who are dependent on their donkeys. The charity currently has major projects in Ethiopia, Kenya, Mexico, India and Egypt, as well as in Europe.

The Donkey Sanctuary grew rapidly, and by 1980 over 800 donkeys had been taken into its care. In addition to Slade House Farm, two more farms had been purchased and staff employed to cater for the ever-increasing numbers! *For the Love of Donkeys* covers the growth of the Sanctuary from 1982 to the middle of 1992, when I received my Honorary Doctorate from the University of Glasgow. This book begins in October 1992 with 'a shaking experience'. Now read on …

1 9 9 2
A SHAKING EXPERIENCE

October

The overseas work of the International Donkey Protection Trust gradually increased over the years, and by 1992 we had set up a trial in Egypt to worm donkeys and monitor the effects. Helping us with this trial was Dr Mourad Ragheb, whom I met through the World Health Organisation, and who had earlier been at the Sanctuary on a training course. He was very keen to help donkeys in Egypt. The trial was successful in proving the benefits of ridding donkeys of internal parasites and so we decided to commence working there as soon as possible. We organised a mobile clinic to operate in the Nile Delta, where the donkeys were in an extremely poor condition. October 1992 found myself and June Evers, my friend and colleague, returning to Egypt to finalise the plans. It sometimes takes years to get projects underway in a developing country, due to governmental delays and veterinary problems in the chosen area, and these have to be overcome before work can commence. At that time we hoped to be able to start work within the next month.

June and I were staying at a hotel on the banks of the Nile in Cairo while making the final arrangements and on 12th October, accompanied by a driver and Mourad, we set off at around 6am to visit the chosen sites. When visiting the more remote and depressed areas of a developing country, it is not always easy to find anything suitable to eat (and it is often the safest bet to refrain from eating some of the local delicacies, as our European stomachs don't always take kindly to it!). We arrived back at the hotel at 4pm absolutely famished. The dining room was closed, and the only chance of getting anything to eat was at a small snack bar by the hotel swimming pool. We hurriedly ordered some food and, while I found a table and chair and waited in anticipation, June sat down at the rear of the pool area with her back against a very high wall. Within minutes I was startled when a group of birds in a tree close by suddenly burst into life and rose in a single body from the tree with a tremendous 'whoosh'. At the same moment I felt the ground beneath my chair shake and, as I looked at the swimming pool, the water was beginning to move from side to side. I realised it was an earthquake and shouted at June to come away from the wall. June was happily reading and, without even looking up, said, 'No, it can't be. They don't have earthquakes in Egypt!' At that moment, the water from the pool sloshed out over the side and poured towards June. She jumped to her feet and, with great difficulty, staggered across to join me on the heaving ground. I had abandoned the table and chair, which by this time had overturned. There were tremendous screams from some Egyptian women who had been sitting nearby and, to our horror, they threw themselves on the ground and appeared to have fainted in fright!

We watched in dismay as the hotel, which was many storeys high, swayed and a window-cleaner's platform about three-quarters of the way up from the ground, on which two men were perched, swung precariously from the building. Very shortly after the last tremor the water from the Nile slowly rose and washed between the huge boulders, which were the only barrier between the pool area and the river. It ran over the ground, joining the water from the swimming pool. It was quite a frightening experience and, needless to say, we didn't get our food!

At the time we were unaware of the extent of the damage. Our driver was unable to take us back to the project the following day, as his daughter was injured during the earthquake while scrambling to evacuate her school. When we were eventually able to get back to work, we saw that many buildings had collapsed, and the driver had to make various detours to avoid areas that were completely blocked. Fortunately Mourad and his family came through unscathed but, like us, they were extremely shaken.

November

During the year I'd decided it would be a good idea for me to invest in a property as, of course, I live in a house owned by the Donkey Sanctuary in order to be on hand for the donkeys, and in the event of my retirement I will probably have to leave it. June and I suffered many disturbed nights due to frequent false alarms warning of fire in the barns. The problem was that, on very cold nights, if a donkey relieved itself under one of the heat sensors, the ensuing warm steam set the alarms off, and I felt I had spent far too many nights rushing out in my night-clothes only to find a donkey with a contented look on its face!

I was looking forward to the odd peaceful night away from the fire alarms. I have always loved the sea and thought it would be a good idea to purchase a flat in a new block which had been built a couple of years previously on the sea front at Sidmouth. I was well into the negotiations to buy a flat, when the vendors lost the property they wished to purchase and withdrew from the sale. I was very disappointed, but the agents put me in touch with the owner of a top floor flat overlooking the sea, and we were soon able to arrange a mutually agreeable figure. This flat was even better than my first choice, which was on the side of the block without a clear sea view. Soon after my return from Egypt the flat became mine.

Both June and the Sanctuary's Deputy Administrator, Brian Bagwell, agreed with me that the high balcony wall restricted the sea view while sitting in the lounge, and Brian had the brilliant idea of raising the floor. This was a tremendous improvement. June and I were looking forward to our first night at the flat but to our horror we'd only just got to sleep when all the fire bells went off and, once again, there I was – out in the cold night air in my dressing gown! Although I've owned the flat for over ten years now, I've spent only that night in it, but it has been worth its weight in gold, because my family can stay there whenever they visit. With four boisterous dogs and two cats in the house, as well as long working hours, get-togethers are much more relaxing and enjoyable now the family has a base close by.

December

During our cruise just before Christmas 1992 June and I visited the Turks and Caicos Islands at the request of the government and the local people, as they had a problem with feral donkeys on the island of Grand Turk. In the past donkeys were used to carry salt from the lakes on the island, but they were abandoned when the commercial viability of the industry failed. They had been left to roam and reproduce freely, but they always had difficulty in finding water during the dry season, and had now started wandering into the town to find food and water. The clever donkeys soon worked a few things out which made government action imperative.

Each house, by law, had to collect any rainfall during the year, and they have plastic drainpipes from their roofs leading into metal water storage tanks. The donkeys had worked out that if they kicked together hard enough at the plastic pipe leading into the tank a miracle occurred – there was water for all! Of course this wasn't satisfactory for the property owners and it was with great regret that they asked their governor to solve the problem. Unfortunately, his answer was to ship all the donkeys to Haiti for meat, which the people were not happy about.

When we arrived we found the donkeys were wild and practically impossible to handle, and many were suffering from sores and parasites. Following meetings with government officials it was agreed that, with the assistance of our funding, a large area of land would be fenced, shelter and water provided and all the donkeys would be rounded up and brought into the compound. It was also agreed that we would find a local person to look after them. An important job for us, however, was to castrate as many stallions as possible to prevent further breeding. We returned home happy in the knowledge that the problems on Grand Turk were being resolved.

1   9   9   3
D O N K E Y S   A N D
O T H E R   A N I M A L S

January

One of my first visits of the year was to a zoo that had a full-bred Poitou stallion. The Poitou donkeys at the Sanctuary were owned by the Slade Centre, and I was not only keen to help continue the line of this rare breed of donkeys, but I felt it was possible that these large 'giants', who stand up to 15 hands high, might be useful in the Centre for larger children to ride. Unfortunately at the time many of this breed were being born with congenital weaknesses in the spine and legs. I was eager to see this donkey to establish his good health and blood line to see if he would be suitable to sire a foal out of our full-bred Poitou mare, Danielle.

The zoo was closed for the winter, and the weather was bitterly cold and frosty when I arrived early in the morning. I was taken to see the donkey by the owner of the zoo, and I was pleased with what I saw. He had all the characteristics of the breed, including long matted hair, and he appeared to be suitable for our purposes. The zoo owner and I discussed arrangements to bring the donkey to the Sanctuary when we felt the time was right.

On the way back to my car I passed the monkey compound which had recently been extended to encompass a small lake. In the middle of the lake was an island, complete with trees, which was reached by a little bridge. A tall pole holding the security lights and cameras was erected on the island, and I was puzzled to see three or four of the zoo's staff standing around the pole holding outstretched nets and gazing upwards. I enquired what the problem was, and was quite amused to hear that, on letting the monkeys into the new area the previous day, they decided that the highest place was the most interesting and they'd all shinned up the pole – right to the very top – and were sitting on the crossbar which held the lights and cameras. Despite all the encouragement with food and kind words, they had refused to come down! The weather was so cold that they were all shivering violently and, one by one, were falling from the pole. It was a wonderful sight to see, as not one of the monkeys actually reached the ground – the staff had managed to catch every one in the net as it fell!

The same cold weather was affecting the Sanctuary. We had long been concerned that some of our donkeys, particularly the elderly or frail ones, lost body condition in the cold winter months, and in response to an earlier appeal we were delighted by people's generosity in sending us money to buy warm, waterproof rugs. The wearing of these, as well as giving extra feed, helped these donkeys enormously, particularly those with medical conditions. We had also launched an appeal for infra-red lights which were fitted overhead in the barns as a heat source that produced a lovely warm glow. The elderly donkeys in New Barn at Slade House Farm were the first to benefit, followed by most of the other barns on the farms where there were sick donkeys or those with special needs.

A new arrival had a particularly sad story. Little Thomas was separated from his mother in a sale at a market when he was only four weeks old. Sadly, we never heard what happened to his mother. She would probably have been in a very stressed condition, as she would have still been feeding her foal when he was taken away from her. Thomas was bought by gypsies and taken to their camp where there was no shelter for him. Neither was there any fencing, and he was tethered around the neck by a chain so heavy he was unable to lift his head. Fortunately for Thomas he was spotted by two animal lovers, who visited and fed him whenever they could, while trying to negotiate

Thomas

his release from the gypsies. Eventually succeeding, they immediately contacted the Sanctuary and asked us to take him into our care.

Everyone had assumed that Thomas was eight to ten months old, but on arrival at the Sanctuary we quickly realised just how young he was. I was absolutely horrified as I watched him. He stood with his head down and showed no signs of the playful antics associated with foals of his age. As the days passed, however, he began to perk up and we put him in a group with mares and their foals. Although the Sanctuary has a 'no breeding' policy, some mares come into our care already in foal, and at this time we had several foals. Donkeys must be the most loving and gentle creatures nature has created because the mares took Thomas under their wing, and even allowed him to suckle occasionally. He didn't stay lost and bewildered for very long and, at the time of writing this book, he is undergoing training to become part of our Show Team.

February

Readers who have supported the Donkey Sanctuary for several years will probably be aware of a most disturbing event which takes place every Shrove Tuesday in the small town of Villanueva de la Vera in Spain. This is the annual festival of Pero Palo, and part of the 'celebrations' involve dragging a donkey around the streets by a rope, with the donkey carrying a man on its back. Hundreds of people throng the streets, many of them in a drunken state, and the donkey is crushed by the weight of people who push and pull at him as they try to pull the man from his back. The roar of the crowd and the sound of guns being fired into the air makes the noise unbearable. The donkey frequently stumbles and falls onto the cobbled streets, and each time it is dragged to its feet by its flesh and hair. Sometimes the donkey falls as many as twenty or thirty times during the two-and-a-half-hour ordeal. By the time the procession has finished the poor animal is absolutely terrified and suffering from severe stress as well as physical injury.

We had been doing our best to stop this dreadful event since we'd heard, in 1986, that a donkey had died in the Fiesta that year, and in 1987 we funded a fervent animal lover, Vicki Moore, to attend the Fiesta. As a result, the *Star* newspaper had bought the donkey (the aims of our charity prohibited us from doing so), and he was brought back to the Sanctuary. Named 'Blackie Star', he was now living in peace and contentment with Lola, to whom Blackie had become attached on his arrival.

The cruel 'celebrations' at Villanueva.

Of course Blackie and Lola were very popular with our visitors and the staff of the Information Centre were often asked questions about them. I think my favourite was when Sydney Judge was asked by an elderly lady, 'Do I understand that Blackie is Spanish?' Syd confirmed that he was. 'Do I understand Lola is Welsh?' the lady asked. 'That's right, madam,' replied Syd. 'So how do they communicate?' she enquired. Syd quickly replied, 'Well – Lola nags him in Welsh and Blackie ignores her in Spanish!'

We had campaigned in every way we could to bring the Fiesta to the attention of anyone who could use their influence to stop it. We had written to members of our Royal Family, King Juan Carlos of Spain and his wife, Queen Sophia, the Spanish Ambassador in London, the Mayor of the town, and to the Pope. In addition, we had also sent letters

Blackie and Lola.

to every householder in the village asking them not to take part. This was all to no avail – the dreadful event took place each year.

We continued with the campaign, however, and in February, in response to our invitation, the publicity officer of Villanueva de la Vera visited the Sanctuary. We were able to demonstrate how happy and contented Blackie Star now was, and she agreed to try to persuade the townspeople of Villanueva de la Vera to consider the welfare of the poor donkeys used in the Fiesta. We felt it was a successful visit, and hoped that, from then on, improvements would be made. In fact this year a genuine attempt was made to protect the donkey, named Misty, although the team present still felt that the treatment he received was unacceptable. He fell six times during the procession but, although at the end his heart rate was very high, Misty had no obvious wounds.

Being a trained teacher, I had always been interested in helping children, and in particular those with special needs and disabilities. In 1975 I had registered a charity known as The Slade Centre, with the aims and objects of giving children with special needs the opportunity to ride and have contact with donkeys. Initially a mobile unit was sent out to special schools in the area, but eventually we were able to build a Centre in the grounds of the Donkey Sanctuary. Children were brought to the Centre by a minibus fitted with a hydraulic platform to enable wheelchairs to be taken on board. The Centre was a success from the outset, with a full complement of children attending on a regular basis. I always felt it was a shame that families were not able to see their child's newly acquired riding skills, so in 1993 we started a Saturday Club which enabled families to attend the Centre to watch the riding sessions and join in the fun. It's wonderful to see the pride in the children's faces as they show off their skills to parents and siblings, and it boosts their confidence enormously. In addition to the work at the Centre a mobile unit was started again this year, taking two or three donkeys in a small lorry to special schools in the area whose curriculum prohibited their attending the Centre. The loving contact with the donkeys, and the skills learned, are seldom forgotten.

The Slade Centre was so successful that I knew there must be thousands of other children around the country who would benefit from the opportunity to get close to a cuddly, friendly donkey and gain therapeutic riding skills. However, the Slade Centre's objects restricted its work to a 25-mile radius of the Sanctuary, and so in 1989 I had set up The Elisabeth Svendsen Trust for Children and Donkeys (EST). This charity had similar objectives to the Slade Centre but it enabled us to set up centres in major cities in the UK. Having established that there was quite a large number of special schools in the Birmingham area, I set up a mobile unit and started looking for a site for EST's first Centre.

For a while I was a Trustee of the Queensway Trust, a charity dealing with deprived children and young offenders, and the Trust had helped with donkey projects in the Birmingham area in an attempt to show young people a different way of life. Sue Brennan worked for the Trust, looking after the donkeys, and Bert Duncan, our Regional Welfare Officer, had also been involved. I was very impressed with Sue's work and was pleased when, following a selection process, she was employed as Principal of the proposed Centre. It wasn't long before the mobile unit had a full schedule of schools to visit. Bert also had good contacts within Birmingham City Council and he approached these on our behalf.

Mrs Barbara Abercrombie is a very keen supporter of our charities. I first met her when she attended our Donkey Week in 1987 and we became good friends. During Donkey Week she had, in fact, met her late companion, Tom Evans. Barbara was very keen that the Birmingham area should be the first to benefit from a new Centre, and she very kindly offered the use of a field on her farm near Birmingham. The site was in a beautiful location, but unfortunately there was a problem with access and for practical reasons I had to turn it down. So it was back to the drawing board!

March

In the course of my work for the Donkey Sanctuary I attend many receptions and events and, at a reception in London held in honour of Organisations Representing Disabled People, I was fortunate to meet the Right Honourable Nicholas Scott, MBE, MP, from the Ministry of Social Security and Disabled People, and Denis Howell MP. I was delighted to have the opportunity to talk to them both for a short time regarding my hopes for EST, and I'm quite sure that the advice and encouragement given to me by both these gentlemen helped me press forward in my endeavours – in fact they may have been instrumental in encouraging Birmingham City Council to come to my assistance.

Late in 1992 I had been delighted to receive a magnificent donation for EST from the Elise Pilkington Charitable Trust. Its Administrator, Lord Brentford, had supported the Donkey Sanctuary for several years, and I thought it would be nice to go and thank him personally during my next visit to London. I was very cordially received and, after discussing my plans with him, I was absolutely staggered when, on behalf of the Trust, he offered me the magnificent sum of £250,000 to build a Centre. In addition, the Trust would give an annual grant towards the running costs. I couldn't believe it – my dream was coming true!

I was delighted when Birmingham City Council offered to lease the charity a small part of beautiful Sutton Park, and I thought the path ahead would be smooth. We engaged the services of architects, William Hawkes, Cave-Brown-Cave, planning permission was granted and Greswolde Construction Ltd were ready and waiting to start work. However, despite having been confident that the building work came within our budget, several unforeseen difficulties meant it would cost much more than expected. A simpler building had to be designed and we then had to wait for planning approval again. Despite cutting the costs, a further £90,000 was needed to get the Centre under way. At times like these I always say that I have to get my prayer mat out! The fund-raising programme moved from desperate to frantic, but despite this within a short time the Centre was on its way.

April

It was around this time that we learned about Jack. I suppose it's a common name for a donkey, but this Jack meant a lot to us. He was an eighteen-year-old stallion, and his home was a fuel tank! Jack had spent much of his life tethered all day in a dealer's yard measuring only about 15' by 20', and a hole had been cut in the side of the tank to give him access to the only shelter he had. The yard was surrounded by scrapped cars packed three high. What a life for a donkey! Charlie Courtney, who was our Deputy Chief Welfare Officer, managed to persuade the owner to let him come into the Sanctuary, where he settled really well. He had to be castrated, of course, as, having over 5,600 donkeys at that time, we didn't particularly want the patter of little hooves. After a period in the Isolation Unit, Jack was sent to Brookfield Farm, where he happily joined what we call 'Big Boys Group'.

May

Donkey Week was held in May and was, once again, a great success. Mourad Ragheb came over from Egypt to receive some further training, and I took the opportunity to ask him to give a talk on his work to our 'Donkey Weekers'. He was able to tell them that the first mobile clinic had been so much in demand in the Nile Delta, with hundreds of owners turning up with their donkeys, that a second unit was being set up, with a second vet and a farrier employed to run it. The word had spread fast that no payment was involved for veterinary treatment and that the donkeys, once treated, were already showing substantial signs of improvement.

Sadly, just after Donkey Week Blackie Star died. We took comfort in the fact that he had spent six happy years at the Sanctuary after his horrendous experience in Spain. Lola was devastated to lose him; she had spent all her time with Blackie and missed him dreadfully. We felt it best to introduce her into a larger group to see if she could find another companion – which she did after a few months, transferring her affections to a rather sedate gelding named Mumphrey, who was delighted to become the object of her affections.

June

Having been 'doctored' at the University of Glasgow in 1992, I was pleased to receive an invitation to the Commemoration Day in June. June Evers joined me for what was a wonderful occasion and one that I was able to enjoy, as during the ceremony last year, I was so nervous I hadn't really taken in all that was happening. The day commenced with the professors assembled together in their official robes. The Clerk of the Senate called out the order for the procession and on his command everyone proceeded in a very dignified manner to the chapel, where a special service was held to honour the benefactors of the university. The procession then wound its way to Bute Hall, to the magnificent accompaniment of an organ recital, and everyone took their place for the presentation of those about to be 'doctored'. It was a very moving occasion, with everyone in the coloured robes of their academic degree – I was so pleased that a magnificent red was allocated to the Doctorate of Veterinary Medicine and Surgery!

In 1987 I had set up a small sanctuary on the island of Lamu, just off the Kenyan coast. During a holiday there a few earlier I had been amazed to see that donkeys were the only form of transport through the very narrow streets of the small town. Everything had to be carried on the donkeys' backs, including heavy building materials, and the donkeys were in a terrible condition, thin and emaciated, and often with badly infected wounds. After a hard day's work their only food supply seemed to be the rubbish tips. Now, under the managership of Abdalla Hadi Rifai, who had first introduced himself to me as a tourist guide, and with regular visits by teams from the UK to carry out worming and veterinary treatment, the condition of the donkeys on Lamu and the surrounding islands was gradually improving.

On our visit to Lamu in 1993 we were accompanied by a film crew from Nairobi who came with us on the long and difficult walk from Faza to Chundwa, two neighbouring islands, where we were going to worm the donkeys. A very muddy estuary had to be crossed by a bridge that was rapidly falling to pieces. Struggling over the bridge one of the crew looked down to see hundreds of crabs moving on the mud. They are an unusual type of crab, having one very large claw and one tiny one. The photographer was fascinated by this, and he asked why they only had one claw. Trying to keep a straight face I told him that they were a source of food for the local villagers and of course if they took both claws the crabs would not survive, so they just took one. The photographer completely swallowed this story and June and I were amused to hear him recounting it to the producer who, thankfully, started laughing immediately!

Our project in Mexico had started as long ago as 1983, thanks to the assistance of Dr Aline de Aluja and her success in persuading the University of Mexico to co-operate with us on a joint project. Initially a mobile unit was started, travelling to villages around Mexico City to treat the donkeys and mules. However there were also hundreds of horses needing help and in 1990 we were pleased to be joined by the International

San Bernabe market.

League for the Protection of Horses, and a second mobile clinic began work.

Everyone was concerned and appalled by the treatment of donkeys and horses at the market in San Bernabe in Mexico, where the equines were bought and sold for slaughter. The poor animals arriving at the market were in a terrible condition. So many were crammed in the lorries that, when opened, these revealed suffocating animals including foals, many trampled underfoot, and others with the most terrible broken legs with open fractures. Many animals were barely alive, but were then forced to jump as much as four feet onto a bank, where they frequently fell and lay in agony for hours, until they were loaded back onto the purchasers' lorries. Our vets were often threatened by the owners of the animals when trying to help the sick and injured donkeys. The whole thing was very upsetting and it was difficult to see what could be done to help, but we thought that perhaps the market owners would accept ramps which we had designed, that could be moved from lorry to lorry, to eliminate the need for the animals to make that awful jump. When my son, Paul, visited the market this year he was delighted to see that several of these ramps were in use. However, the problems with the market were far from being resolved.

Just as we do for the donkey owners on Lamu, a competition for the

Competition for the best kept donkey in Mexico.

best kept horse, mule and donkey was held in two villages in Mexico. Dr Aline was absolutely amazed that in one village there were 68 equines and in the other a staggering 183! The judges had a very difficult task. Prizes were given to the winning owners, together with protective backpacks for the equines. At last it seemed that owners were showing pride in the fact that their equines were healthy.

July

Back at the Sanctuary I was interested to meet two new arrivals – a donkey named Paddy and his companion. Our policy at the time was to take into our care companion animals to donkeys, but only when it was obvious that there was a definite bond with the donkey. A strange assortment of animals has been acquired for this reason, including chickens, ducks, goats, ponies and horses, and they are all afforded the same privileges as the donkeys – love, care and attention for the rest of their natural lives, and only put down when their quality of life has come to an end. Paddy's inseparable companion was a new one to us – Crumble was a large Jersey-cross cow (see picture on p 17). Paddy, who was over 40, had lived with his friend for more than 20 years and we were told that they were both going to be shot if a new home wasn't found for them. So in they came, and they were a constant source of amusement to everyone; Paddy stood happily while Crumble licked him constantly with her long rough tongue – he loved it! We had to allocate them special quarters in the Isolation Unit, as not all our shelters could accommodate such a large friend!

The Donkey Sanctuary is often featured in both local and national press. Normally it is very complimentary and appreciative of the work we do, but in July we were dismayed to read an article by Auberon Waugh in the *Daily Telegraph* entitled 'A use for donkeys'. He was highly critical of our work, describing the Sanctuary as 'one of the saddest sights in Europe, after the War Graves in the north of France and Euro Disney at Marne-la-Vallée, with more than 5,000 donkeys hanging around in forlorn groups with nothing to do and looking useless'. He wondered why donkeys should be more fortunate than redundant British workers at a time of world recession, adding that donkeys were intractable and obdurate animals by nature and it was often necessary to beat them severely before they could be persuaded to perform the simplest tasks. He finished the article by saying that if the government was serious in its plans to allow education to occur once again in schools, it might be a good idea to put donkeys into all the teacher training colleges for trainee teachers to practise on.

Apparently hundreds of people wrote letters in protest at his words, as later that month another article appeared headed 'Donkeys to the rescue'. He admitted that his letterbox had been filled for several days with letters from donkey lovers complaining about his article. He understood that, far from standing around with nothing to do all day, the donkeys were regularly visited and ridden by children with special needs, and appeared at shows giving exhibitions. He said he recognised the enthusiasm and exuberance of donkey-fanciers, who described them as beautiful, brave, kind, loyal, brilliantly clever, industrious, articulate, honest, thrifty and endowed with a keen sense of moral priorities. Many supporters had taken exception to his comments and he said that, under the circumstances, perhaps he ought to amend his recommendation. He ended with appropriate apologies to the donkeys of the world and their admirers. He said that perhaps they should go as professors to teach the elements of good manners, reading, writing, arithmetic, English, history, French and Latin, from the store of their wisdom, to the almost totally ignorant generation which sought to educate our children at the moment.

I was so grateful to all those who wrote letters of protest to him. There must have been so many that he felt he should offer some sort of apology, albeit a veiled one!

August

Over the past few years I had attended the biennial Conference of the World Association for the Advancement of Veterinary Parasitology (WAAVP), which was held in a different country each time. This year the conference was held in the UK, the venue being in Cambridge. I was pleased to see that donkeys were included on the agenda and I was asked to chair a section in a workshop based on donkeys and their problems worldwide. It was good to know that the welfare of donkeys was at last being considered as important.

September

A strange request awaited me on my return to the Sanctuary. The Rag Morris Men from Bristol asked if they could come and do some dancing in the Main Yard. This was for their own entertainment, although obviously they would catch the eye of visitors at the time. I felt it would be a new cultural experience for the donkeys, who are free to roam around the yard during the day and mingle with the visitors. I felt sure everyone would enjoy it. It was true that the donkeys were absolutely fascinated, and they watched the first dance with much curiosity. However, they disappeared very quickly into their stables when the Rag Morris Men did their stick dance. The sound of the sticks being struck together must have stirred memories in some of them; only a few brave but anxious donkeys peered out to see what would happen next! Understanding the problem, the dancers refrained from doing that type of dance again. It was a rather interesting afternoon for donkeys and visitors alike.

October

I've always believed that all animal charities should work together and we co-operate closely with many of them, realising how useful it is to share ideas in order to help animals in the best possible way. It was for this reason that CEBEC (Chief Executives of British Equine Charities) was established. Our meetings have no fixed agenda, although each member suggests a particular topic, which is discussed in a frank and constructive manner by all present. Such topics have included various equine welfare issues, Charity Commission regulations, tax implications and charity trading. Meetings are held twice yearly, and occasionally a VIP, often a government minister, is invited to join us for lunch. The information gained on the latest government thinking with regard to equine welfare can be invaluable. At our meeting in October I was interested to meet Nicholas Soames MP and hear his views on animal welfare.

I was honoured once again to receive an invitation to the Women of the Year Luncheon at the Savoy Hotel in London. I was first invited to this annual event in 1989 and thoroughly enjoyed meeting some of the most interesting women from many aspects of life, from theatre to business. Princess Margaret was this year's Guest of Honour, and I was delighted to have the opportunity to speak to her for a few moments. At each table were approximately eight people, and everyone was presented with souvenir items including a 'telephone card' which I have since discovered is a collector's item. It was nice to think that my work for animals was being recognised, and I wore my uniform each time, as I felt it was the donkeys who were being honoured rather than me. Anyway, I prefer my working shoes to high heels.

November

Normally my visits overseas are fraught with difficulties, working mainly in areas where tourists don't go and staying in accommodation

CREALY COUNTRY
Devonshire

TORTOISE MOT TEST RESULTS

Name	ROGA
Sex	FEMALE
Species	SPURTHIGHED
Weight	1800g
Carapace length	204 mm
Age	50
Condition	Very Good .
Hibernation	3 months maximum
Date	24.10.93
Examined by	Weekes .

For more information and advice, contact Helen at Crealy Country ☎ 0395 233200.

Roga's MOT.

which is often not very clean. It's very easy to pick up infections, not only from the food but also from the many insects that enjoy a bite of one's flesh! A visit to Jersey was a refreshing change, although the reason was a sad one. I went to attend the funeral of my old friend, Kitty Massey. I first met Kitty when I visited Jersey many years before to give a lecture. She had shown great enthusiasm for my work, and soon became a supporter of the Sanctuary and a good friend. I learned of her death with great sorrow and decided that I would attend her funeral in Jersey. I'd also been advised that Kitty had left me a legacy in her Will – her cat, Feather, and her tortoise, Roga!

Both the burial service and the interment were very sad. It was absolutely pouring with rain but the little church was beautiful and I'm sure Kitty would have enjoyed the service. I was very pleased to meet Kitty's relatives, Tim and Jane Wiener, who later became supporters of the Sanctuary; as I left, they handed Feather and Roga to me for the return journey. As I already had two cats myself I felt unable to have Feather at home, but a member of the Sanctuary's staff agreed to take her. I decided to keep Roga, who was sent to a specialist for an MOT, when I learned 'he' was in fact a 'she', and was about 50 years old (as you will see from the MOT Certificate!). She was a good age and I kept her for several years before she died. After all Kitty's help, I'm pleased to think I was able to fulfil her wishes.

December

June Evers and I again took a Christmas/New Year break, although it was more of a working trip, as we planned to visit Grand Turk to see how the work on the donkey compound was going. We had also arranged to meet with members of the government, in addition to finding suitable local staff to run the project.

January

Things didn't quite go to plan on our proposed visit to Grand Turk. We arrived in Miami to find that the flight to Providenciales (one of the group of Turks and Caicos Islands) had been cancelled. We spent over eleven hours at Miami airport trying to find another way to get there, but the only flight possible was already fully booked and there was no guarantee of a return flight. Regretfully we had to cancel the trip, but I was able to discuss the project with Gail Johnston who had been keeping an eye on the situation for us. She advised me that the compound had been fenced and water troughs installed, and the next step would be to round up all the feral donkeys on the island. We would then have to arrange for the stallions to be castrated to prevent problems in the future, and I advised Gail that I would return later in the year.

We returned to the Sanctuary in time to see the arrival of Dinky, who had the dubious honour of being our 6,000th admission! I didn't know whether we should be laughing or crying as he came down the ramp with his Shetland pony companion, Miner (picture on previous page). Press photographers crowded around a rather unwilling 35-year-old celebrity! I didn't really think there were so many donkeys in the UK when I started, and I began to wonder how many there were left.

Dinky's story is a lovely one. At one stage he was a well known character in Durham, where he visited the market-place pulling a smart little trap, and he was especially popular at Christmas. He was purchased in 1969, at the age of about 10, as a birthday present for a lady from her husband, and had a loving and happy home with the family. Unfortunately for Dinky the family had to move abroad, so they sent him into our care, saying, 'We need to know he will be properly looked after in his old age.'

Dinky was quite a character, and had become an expert escapologist, rolling under wire fences, visiting the house, and even climbing up steep stairs in a barn to reach the new season's hay (it took four men to get him down!). When we found that Dinky had lived for most of his life with Miner, a Shetland pony, we agreed to take him in as well. It would have caused both a lot of stress if they had been separated. Dinky enjoyed his last years at the Sanctuary in happy retirement until his death in September 1996, aged 37 years. Miner stayed at the Sanctuary until he died in 1998.

Together with the International League for the Protection of Horses, we had organised a petition to stop the live export of donkeys for slaughter, which we planned to present to the President of the European Parliament in Strasbourg later in the year. We also asked our supporters to write letters of protest to their Euro MPs. We suspected for some time that donkeys were being transported from Ireland, destined for the meat market in Europe. Thousands of animals were leaving Ireland every year, some travelling vast distances for slaughter. Ireland was known as the 'back door' for many exporters as it was so easy for dealers to get animals out of the country. Paul received a tip-off that a load of donkeys had been discovered in a closed van and small trailer on the ferry en route from Rosslare to Le Havre. An enquiring deck-hand had heard strange noises coming from the vehicle and had managed to see the donkeys through a crack in the door. The only way Paul could get to the docks in time to stop the vehicle was to charter a plane from Exeter, at a staggering cost of £1,200! Determined to help, we rang the *Mail on Sunday*, who said they would pay the air fare and publish the story.

The French authorities were initially very helpful, detaining the vehicle until Paul and his colleagues arrived. On inspecting the donkeys in the vehicle they were appalled – the transport of donkeys in this way contravened nearly all the transport rules and regulations. Ten of the donkeys were crammed into the small trailer, which was dripping with condensation as there was no ventilation. Although there was hay, it could be reached by only a few of the donkeys and it was impossible for the others to move nearer to it as they were packed in so tightly. In the van they found a further three donkeys partitioned in a small area. The donkeys were held in French quarantine facilities for one week. They were housed in a large barn and were fed and watered. Had the journey continued without our intervention their total journey time to their final destination would have been in excess of 48 hours.

We hoped the donkeys would be confiscated and we could get them away, but it was not to be. Our staff sat and waited day after day, pleading with the authorities to let us take the donkeys until, finally, they were loaded onto the van and driven off despite our protests. We followed the donkeys from France all the way through to their final destination – which was in Germany. The people transporting the donkeys told us they were going to a farm where children could cuddle and ride them. However, when we visited the farm, the donkeys had disappeared and the only clues as to where they had ended up, sadly, led to a huge abattoir or a tannery factory. We immediately wrote to the Directorate-General for Agriculture at the European Commission, who initiated legal proceedings against Ireland in respect of their failure to adopt as National Law Directive 91/628/EEC relating to the protection of animals during transport.

We also received reports that double-decker lorries with up to a hundred donkeys and horses on board were travelling from Portugal to Belgium, and a team from the Donkey Sanctuary followed them. Again, this was reported to the European Commission. A reply was received that they were drawing the attention of the Belgian authorities to the Commission's Directive prohibiting the carrying of solipeds (the general name for all equines) in double-decker vehicles.

While I suppose in principle there is no reason why donkey meat should not be eaten in the same way as that of other animals, we felt that journeys in such lorries for up to 48 hours at a time without food, water or rest periods were inhumane, and we were desperate to have legislation improved for the welfare of animals during transportation – conditions for animals can be so cruel, and I do get very upset at times.

One of our new arrivals should have been a more fortunate little donkey! She lived in the grounds of a public house and, had she been in view, she probably would have been thoroughly spoilt by the regulars. Sadly though, Holly lived in a field behind the pub and she'd not had many visitors. When the pub changed hands the new owners didn't even know of her existence for two whole months, by which time she had become very thin and was infested with lice. Having not been cleaned out for so long, the dung in Holly's shelter had built up so high that her head was almost touching the roof, and her field was full of ragwort. Ragwort is terribly dangerous to equines and very often the effects of eating it, particularly after it has flowered and dried off, don't become apparent for two or three years. The effects of ragwort poisoning are irreversible. A medical examination on Holly's arrival revealed no signs of ragwort poisoning but after three happy years at the Sanctuary she sadly developed severe eye problems, and had to be euthanased.

February

This month brought the dreaded Fiesta in Villanueva de la Vera once again. Misty, the donkey used last year, was again put through the horrific ordeal. Our team was allowed to examine Misty both before and after the event and, although perhaps there was a slight improvement on former years, and very brave efforts made by local

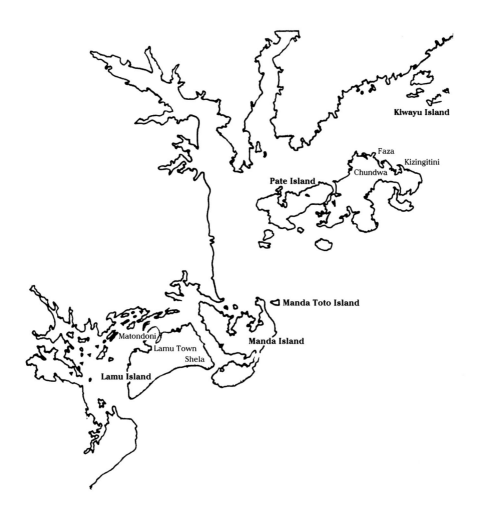

Lamu and other islands along the Kenyan coast.

villagers to protect him, Misty still fell several times, and was extremely stressed and frightened.

Visits to Kenya by a team from the Sanctuary to worm the donkeys were continuing. The journey to Lamu entails an hour-and-a-half flight from Nairobi to a landing strip on Manda Island which is across the estuary from Lamu. Once there, trips to the neighbouring islands to worm the donkeys and give any necessary advice involve long days and arduous journeys. The time of departure by boat from Lamu is dependent on the tides, as we have to travel up a narrow estuary between the mainland and Manda Island, and there is a shallow area about halfway along which dries up at low tide. We therefore have to make sure that we reach what is known as 'elephant crossing' at high tide to enable the boat to go through. Both sides of the estuary are covered in thick jungle and mangroves, and elephant crossing is named for obvious reasons. On arriving at one of the islands we often have to walk as much as 8 miles after leaving the boat to get to the various villages, and don't return to Lamu until sometimes as late as 8 or 9 o'clock in the evening, depending on the tides.

On one trip we knew we would not have time to do all our work in one day since, as well as Pate, Chundwa and Faza, we also had to visit Kizingitini and Kiwayu Island. There was a hotel at Kizingitini and we arranged to stay there for the night. Landing from the boat was precarious to say the least – there was a heavy swell running and we were almost thrown out of the small motor boat several times. When we eventually staggered ashore we were soaked through. The accommodation was in little huts thatched with makuti (a type of reed) and the windows were simply holes cut in the side of the huts. June and I were desperate for a shower, which was situated at the back of the building. It consisted of a rope which had to be pulled to release the water from above. It reminded me of a story Bill Jordan, one of our Trustees, had told me. He had been using a similar shower when, on pulling the rope, no water was forthcoming. Looking up into the dark roof space he saw, sitting on the rafters, a small boy who shrugged and said, 'No more water in the bucket, master' !

Having showered, I found June examining a large ottoman at the foot of the bed, which was just large enough to hold two people. 'I've been told that we should get in here if we hear a lion approaching,' she said, and we both laughed! The stay was nevertheless very unusual – during the night monkeys entered the hut and stole all our make-up from the dressing table, and in the morning we discovered some definite snake tracks around the hut!

Getting back on the boat proved just as difficult, but we managed to keep our veterinary equipment dry and landed safely on the tiny island of Kiwayu. There we found a donkey that had been attacked by a lion, which had apparently swum across from Kizingitini! The villagers had managed to frighten the lion back into the sea with gunshots, but the poor donkey had terrible injuries to its hindquarters. As the Muslim religion prohibits euthanasia, we were only able to give the donkey painkillers and, mercifully, it died shortly afterwards. On the return journey we only just managed to get through elephant crossing as darkness fell, and we were so pleased to get back to the Peponi Hotel where a hot shower and a good dinner were waiting!

Talking of elephants reminds me of an earlier visit to Lamu. Taking off from the airstrip is always rather tricky, as the runway is quite short and only very small planes are used. On this particular occasion I was sitting in the front of a tiny Piper plane next to the pilot, with Bill Jordan sitting behind us. The pilot accelerated down the runway, only to suddenly slam on the brakes, causing the plane to nearly slew off the runway into the bushes. I looked at him and asked what the problem was, to which he replied, 'Elephant dung on the runway.' 'Couldn't we have gone through it?' I asked, quite surprised. He looked at me rather condescendingly and said, 'Where there's elephant dung, there are elephants, and it's quite possible that some will be crossing the runway at any second.' I shrunk back in my seat feeling really embarrassed as we taxied back to the beginning of the runway to wait for a while before starting again. I hoped that on our future trips there wouldn't be any elephant dung on the runway, and decided that I certainly wouldn't ask any questions again.

We received so many reports from members of the public with regard to donkeys in poor condition or circumstances they had seen whilst on holiday in different parts of the world that we decided to set up a 'World Donkey Survey'. People travelling abroad could apply to the Sanctuary for an information pack complete with map, information sheets and advice on donkey welfare. We were also very concerned about the use of 'donkey taxis' in various parts of Spain, particularly in Mijas, as well as on some of the Greek islands. Katie Boyle, a loyal supporter of our work, very kindly offered to advise listeners to her regular radio programme of our work, and pointed out how useful any information received could be in assisting our charity to help the donkeys.

March

One interesting visitor this month was Sandra Pady, who was in the process of setting up the Donkey Sanctuary of Canada. Sandra felt that the best place she could learn about running an animal charity was with us, and she eagerly visited the different departments to see how we operated. We also organised a training session so Sandra could learn how to catch and handle donkeys. I was able to give her advice on how to set up and run a charity and the best way to raise funds, and also advised her of the problems she might face when taking into care large numbers of donkeys. Sandra is a very nice lady and I believe that her organisation is running successfully.

April

Accompanied by Paul and June, I attended the 2nd International Colloquium for Working Equines in Rabat in Morocco. This meeting covered all aspects of donkeys, mules and horses in tropical agricultural development, from nutrition, harnessing and health to psychology, and was a really interesting meeting. It was a wonderful opportunity for our vets to join other vets from around the world so that we could all get together to discuss equine problems and exchange information. Joining us were Michael Crane, one of the vets from Ikin and Oxenham, the local practice that was then in charge of the donkeys at the Sanctuary; Dr Aline de Aluja, Co-ordinator of our Mexican project, with Alfredo and Horacio, the two vets running the Mexican mobile clinics; Dr Mourad Ragheb, Project Leader in Egypt; Dr Yilma Makonnen, Co-ordinator from the Faculty of Veterinary Medicine in Ethiopia, and Dr Varma from the Kenya Society for the Protection and Care of Animals.

Another vet in attendance was Andrew Trawford. Andrew had worked with me for some years at the Donkey Sanctuary as our senior vet, but had left to further his experience overseas. We have always kept in contact and he kept his eye on donkeys in the countries where he worked. However, Andrew was now interested in returning to the UK and answered our advertisement for a veterinary surgeon. He was the successful candidate and we agreed that he would return to the Sanctuary in October 1994 as Senior Veterinary Surgeon. I really looked forward to his re-joining our team.

Returning from Rabat I was upset to find that poor Timothy was losing his battle for life. Before he came into our care (in 1976), Timothy was attacked by vandals who held him down and chopped off both his ears. This had obviously caused Timothy the utmost pain and distress. On his arrival at the Sanctuary we had considered putting him down for his own benefit, as he was so unhappy and was impossible to handle. However, Herb Fry, my very first employee, took personal care of Timothy and with his patience and gentle care Timothy had slowly settled down, becoming attached to a donkey named Henrietta, and a firm favourite with our many regular visitors. His health had never been particularly good but he had spent many years with us and had reached the ripe old age of forty-three. Even so, losing him was difficult

Timothy with Herb Fry.

to accept. I stayed with him as much as I could over his last few days, but finally I agreed with the vets that he had no quality of life and he should be put to sleep. I was able to hold his head and give him his favourite ginger biscuits whilst the vets carried out their task.

As though to compensate for the loss of Timothy, another donkey with the same name came into the Sanctuary within days! This Timothy had lived in the same home for twenty-five years, having been born there. His mother had died two years earlier and was buried in the donkeys' field. Since then the ponies in the neighbouring field had been moved away, as had the sheep, so Timothy was very lonely. His owners were moving house and with great regret and sadness they felt it was in Timothy's best interests to come into the Sanctuary. They were delighted to learn that, after his initial stay in the Isolation Unit, he was to go to our farm, Three Gates, at Leigh, near Sherborne in Dorset, as they were buying a house in that area and could visit him regularly. A happy ending for all!

May

Donkey Week soon came round again, and all our regular friends turned up, joined by many new visitors for this 'holiday with a difference'. The ages of those attending range from the very young to the very elderly, and many firm friendships are forged during the week. A lot of fun is had by all, and I particularly remember with great fondness the great fun we had when Nick Patrickson was here. Nick and his mother, Marjorie, attended several years running and we were all devastated when we heard that Nick, who was only in his early forties, was diagnosed as suffering from multiple sclerosis. He took his failing health remarkably well but as he grew weaker it was obvious that he couldn't manage to walk around the farms as he used to. He refused to give in to his illness, and didn't want to take up the offer this year of an electric wheelchair which we kept in the Information Centre – until members of the Information Centre's staff, Ron Smith and Dean Hancock, stepped in and challenged Nick to a wheelchair race! I just happened to be walking back from the hospital when I was amazed to see Ron charging around in the wheelchair while Dean timed him with a stopwatch. When Ron finished his circuit, Nick was gently lowered into the wheelchair to have his turn! He enjoyed himself so much that he decided to use the wheelchair for the remainder of the week – and in fact bought it from us before he went home.

Helping other charities can have its problems and we had been

Mal took on the role of naughtiest donkey.

increasingly concerned with regard to a charity called the Cornwall Donkey and Pony Sanctuary, not because of the work they did, which we hoped would be successful, but because many of our supporters were getting confused between the two completely separate organisations. The situation became even more confused when a television channel featured the Cornwall Donkey and Pony Sanctuary, but used archived film footage of our Sanctuary! I hoped that explaining the difference in our Newsletter would clarify the matter.

We always thought that when we lost little Eeyore there would never be such a naughty donkey again, but I think we were all proved wrong. Mal was a dear little colt foal born to Ellen, one of a group of thirty-five donkeys owned by a beach donkey operator in Blackpool. The donkeys had been found living in filthy and over-crowded conditions; they were rescued by the RSPCA and sent by them into our care. I am always so grateful for the co-operation of the RSPCA. We have an understanding that, if their inspectors find donkeys in trouble, and bring a prosecution, the donkeys can be sent into our care until the court case is heard. If a ban on the keeping of animals is imposed, the RSPCA arranges for the donkeys to be relinquished to the Donkey Sanctuary.

At first Mal was rather sickly, which was hardly surprising when you consider the problems his mother had faced whilst carrying him. After a spell in our hospital he recovered from a chest infection and, as he grew, so did his mischievousness. His daily groom was Colette, and she soon learned not to fasten her coat toggles, as he would quietly nuzzle her and then suddenly his little teeth would clamp around a toggle! He would just hang on ... and on ... and on! Colette's only choice was to leave the coat open so that she could slip it off and leave him with it until he tired of the game. His various antics spurred me on to write a new children's story about him, and we combined this with some stories about Eeyore to make a nice hardback edition for children.

June

By the middle of the year I was feeling the need for a holiday and quite by chance I read an article in one of the national papers about gold panning in south-west Scotland. The idea appealed to me, so I wrote to Mr Smart of the Lowther Gold Panning School at Mennock Pass. What a good decision it was! Charlie Smart was a delightful and enthusiastic gold panner and, with his skilled help, June and I spent a wonderful few days wading in the Mennock river in the Lowther hills. We pumped

Gold panning.

out the grit from the bedrock and sifted it through our pans, eagerly looking for tiny pieces of glinting gold! I cannot explain how wonderfully relaxing it was to be standing sometimes knee-deep in beautiful clear running water, finding tiny amounts of gold and, when occasionally we stopped to ease our aching backs, watching kingfishers and other birds and small animals around us. We were amazed to see trout wriggling their way between our feet and playing in the deep holes we were making in the river bed. Charlie had recommended that we stay in Blackaddie House in Sanquhar which we found very comfortable, and the wonderful Scottish kindness and hospitality made our evenings a pleasure. Having been in the river from about 9 o'clock in the morning until 4 in the afternoon, we returned to the hotel soaked through to the skin. Our wet clothes were taken away to dry and we enjoyed a lovely dinner in the evening. The amount of gold collected on this first trip was, of course, minute, but we saved it carefully and after several visits to Scotland we managed to collect enough to have it made into several small items of jewellery.

July

Quietly walking around the Sanctuary is a most enjoyable part of my job. I visit all the barns to check that everything is in order, and I am always accompanied on these occasions by at least half the group of donkeys in the unit, all determined to be touched and stroked. As you can imagine, with over a hundred donkeys sharing a barn, this can take quite a long time. I also enjoy walking around the Memorial Walks, where supporters can arrange for benches and trees to be placed in memory of someone who has died – a member of their family, a friend or often a much-loved pet.

August

At this time the University of Glasgow Veterinary School was in the process of building a new equine welfare centre at the university, which was to be called The Weipers Centre. I agreed to see if I could persuade other equine charities to help with the funding. I had good connections at the veterinary school, including Professor Norman Wright, who was at that time the Dean of the Faculty, Professor Max Murray and Professor Jimmy Duncan. They had always been very helpful, and had undertaken non-intrusive research on the donkey and given us advice whenever needed. The Trustees felt that a centre such as this would be of great value, particularly with regard to the training of vets on our overseas projects, and they decided to pay for the construction of stables for donkeys undergoing treatment. I was delighted to go to Glasgow to present the cheque personally to Professor Wright.

Following my visit to the university I was able to visit Jimmy Duncan at his farm in Biggar. He was very keen on breeding high quality cattle, and I wasn't sure whether or not to feel flattered when he took me to see two newly born calves which he had named 'Betty' and 'Juno'!

September

To my great delight the EST Centre in Sutton Park, Birmingham, was officially opened on 12th September. A wonderful display was put on by children from schools that had previously been visited by our mobile unit in Birmingham, and a coach trip was arranged so that Sanctuary staff could enjoy the day too. It really was such a wonderful moment to see the children enter the Centre for the first time and see the special facilities which meant that their riding sessions could be guaranteed winter and summer alike.

At the Weipers Centre with (left to right) *Professor Max Murray, Professor Norman Wright and Professor Jimmy Duncan.*

The skills that the children learn over the summer can easily be lost again during the winter period, and we were delighted that the children with special needs in the Birmingham area could now enjoy riding donkeys throughout the year. Of course none of this could have happened without the wonderful generosity of The Elise Pilkington Charitable Trust and Birmingham City Council, and a large donation from Sutton Coldfield Municipal Charities was also a great boost to our funds at the time. Although we had sufficient running costs for the first year, it was going to be a challenge to raise enough to continue the Centre's work. I have to say, though, that this didn't stop me planning the next Centre in another city!

EST Centre in Sutton Park, Birmingham.

October

It was during a gentle stroll along one of the Walks that I had the idea of holding a Memorial Day, when all those supporters who had arranged for a memorial to their loved-ones could come together at the Sanctuary and have the opportunity to visit and place flowers next to the plaques, and to attend a service to commemorate the lives of those they had lost. The 4th October is the Feast Day of St Francis of Assisi, the patron saint of animals, and I felt this would be an ideal date to hold this special day. Our local vicar, Reverend Peter Leverton, readily agreed to join us. Following a service in our marquee, with the donkeys joining in with the hymn singing, Reverend Leverton and I were driven around the Sanctuary in what we called 'the popemobile', so that he could bless the memorials and give words of comfort to those present. Everyone who attended was pleased with the day, and we all agreed that Memorial Day should become an annual event.

Paul had been such a wonderful help and support, and I was devastated when he told me that he wanted to leave the Donkey

Sanctuary to set up his own business. I understood his reasons, of course; for a long time he had been interested in film-making and had made some excellent videos for our charities. He now wanted to gain more business experience by setting up a video company in Seaton. I knew I would miss him terribly.

November

In November I accompanied Brian Bagwell, our Deputy Administrator, to Ireland for the official opening of a new clinic, offices and stable area at our Irish Sanctuary in Liscarroll, County Cork. I had heard about Irish ceremonies, but it really is necessary to experience one to fully appreciate the great pleasure the Irish take from an opportunity to celebrate! Literally hundreds of local people turned up, along with the mayor and mayoress of County Cork, the Chairperson of Cork County Council and local officials. We were also honoured when Ted Pinney,

The 'popemobile'.

Chairman of our local East Devon District Council, agreed to come to Ireland with us. I don't think Ted had ever seen anything like it – certainly not in Sidmouth.

December
Our Christmas/New Year cruise this year took us to Antigua, followed by a visit to Grand Turk. I hadn't felt too well while I was away, but I put it down to having eaten something which disagreed with me, and tried my best to enjoy the holiday.

1 9 9 5
ADOPTING A DONKEY

Tom Harrison

Daniel P

Tapestry

Megan

Donk Dean

Pasco

Oscar

Charlie C

January

To my horror, on my return from the cruise, a most intense pain started in my lower left abdomen. I was in such agony I had no choice but to go to the doctor, who immediately referred me to hospital. Within two hours I was admitted and various tests were undertaken which proved quite painful because there had been no time to administer an anaesthetic. I had to spend three days in hospital before being discharged, and was told I would have to return for further X-rays.

I was afraid it was a return of the shigella that I contracted in 1991, but the results showed that this had now developed into diverticulitis which, although controllable by changes to diet, could become acute and persistent and could need to be remedied by surgery. The doctor told me it was important that I should never be too far from medical assistance and, sadly, I realised that my visits to developing countries were now out of the question. I had to accept this as gracefully as I could, consoling myself with the fact that there was still much work to be done in the UK.

With the odd exception, I am pleased to say that the majority of beach operators in the UK care for and look after their donkeys very well. Nora Cleghorn was a kind and caring owner and always had a great love of donkeys. She had operated up to 22 beach donkeys for over 45 years, and at one time had three pitches – at Jaywick, Clacton and St Osythes. Over the years the number of donkeys Nora owned reduced to just 6 operating at Jaywick on Sundays. Nora used to travel by bicycle down to the pitch with her donkeys coming along behind her! However, due to her husband's ill health and her own increasing age, Nora decided the time had come for the last of her donkeys to retire and join the other 14 already taken into the Sanctuary. All the donkeys settled happily into their new environment. Reading through their admission sheets I was amused to read of Sam Cleghorn, 'aged 12 years, no particular medical history, likes lemonade, squash from a cup and children'! Sam arrived with his mother, Sandy Cleghorn, aged 16 years, and other members of the family. This little group of donkeys was kept together during their time in the Isolation Unit, after which they went to Woods Farm, where the rest of Nora's donkeys were residing. It was interesting to note that the first of Nora's donkeys to come in was Katie, number 298, who arrived on 17th September 1975, whereas the date of Sam's arrival was 6th December 1994 and he was number 6,337!

At the end of January I was able to go to Denmark for a few days to see my daughter, Lise, her husband Jan and their children, Mark and Kate. Lise is a qualified teacher and Jan had worked at a hospital in Randers where he gained good management experience. They decided that together they would set up a school teaching English to Danish students as well as supplying schools in Denmark with specialist reading material. Their little business, which they called 'The English Centre', had grown rapidly. I had great fun finding a red telephone kiosk that they could buy to put outside their house to advertise their business, which I arranged to be shipped to Denmark.

February

Returning home I once again became totally immersed in the running of the Sanctuary. Luckily I had a wonderful and dedicated team working with me, who helped me cope with the workload. One particularly busy day was interrupted when my personal assistant, Sue Harland, came into my office to say that an elderly gentleman and his wife wished to see me. I rarely say I'm too busy to see supporters of our charity so, as the lady was disabled and couldn't climb the stairs, I agreed to meet them in the boardroom on the ground floor. After a brief introduction the gentleman advised me that he had designed a special donkey shelter, and promptly produced a very worn and grubby plan, laying it carefully on the table. He proudly explained his design to me and his wife chipped in with odd comments every now and again. I felt rather guilty in telling them how similar his design was to what we were already using. They looked so disappointed and, in an effort to make them feel better I said, 'This plan is rather worn – would you like a copy?' What I had in mind was to provide them with a clean photo copy, but before the gentleman had time to reply his wife leaned across the table and said, 'Oh, yes please, dear – both with two sugars and a little milk!' This misunderstanding cost me almost three-quarters of an hour of valuable time!

The EST Centre in Birmingham was now running very smoothly, and it was amazing to note that by early February it was fully booked up every week by special schools in the area. When visiting with my sister, Pat, I had the opportunity to meet up with Peter Hillcox, the Chief Ranger of Sutton Park, who had been really magnificent in his encouragement and help with starting the Centre in Sutton Park. Peter and his fellow Park Rangers were happy to co-operate in arranging joint events so that the Centre could become an integral part of the facilities available within the Park.

To provide a regular income for the running costs of the Centres, in the previous November I had come up with the idea of an Adoption Scheme, using four selected donkeys from both the Sidmouth and Birmingham Centres. I felt this would be an excellent way to raise funds for EST as well as providing a special interest to our supporters. When Sue Hudson, who was working in my administration office, volunteered to run the scheme, little did she realise how popular the idea would become. For the first six months I often suggested that she should bring her bed into the office. She worked such long hours, there was almost no time to go home! Since the scheme started, thousands of supporters have 'adopted' their own special donkey, perhaps for themselves or as a gift to a loved-one or friend; everyone receives a certificate and a photograph of their chosen donkey. Many people turn up at the Centres to see their donkeys, bringing them carrots and polo mints – a good time is had by all.

Following the visit to Birmingham, June joined me and together we travelled up to Scotland where we spent another delightful three days searching for gold. It was very different from our last visit in September, when the only problem we encountered had been mosquitoes. This time the weather was bitterly cold and we were a bit disconcerted to see icicles hanging from the rocks and heather alongside the now fast-running brook. I have to admit it wasn't very pleasant to stand in the knee-deep holes we had dug, with our hands beneath the freezing water, but to our great delight June soon found what could only be described as a small nugget! Encouraged by the exciting 'find', we carried on regardless, but unfortunately this was the only gold we found during the whole three days! I can't remember ever feeling so cold as we did on returning to the hotel each evening!

The Fiesta in Villanueva de la Vera loomed again. This year Misty was not used, as he had gone lame. We were pleased that the chosen donkey, whose name we did not establish, was much larger and stronger. He didn't fall during the procession and, although he was deeply stressed, the team was able to examine him after his ordeal and was reasonably satisfied with his condition, although we were told that he showed signs of uncontrollable behaviour later. I immediately wrote to the Spanish Ambassador and the relevant Spanish authorities to express our gratitude for the improvements made, hoping that these would continue. We also arranged a meeting with the villagers to continue the pressure to stop the Fiesta or at least to put the donkey at the head of the procession.

March

All donkeys seem to love ginger nut biscuits and, although we're aware that these are not particularly good for their teeth, they are given as an occasional special treat. They are also very useful when the donkeys need to have medication which, when sandwiched between two ginger nuts, they eat without a second thought! In the Spring Newsletter I asked if anyone could supply us with these biscuits at a reduced rate or – even better – free! We were absolutely amazed at the response – we received hundreds of packets from our supporters, plus 24 cases from Fox's Biscuits, 10 kilos from Elkes Biscuits and nearly half a ton from McVitie's! As you can imagine, the donkeys were delighted!

The project in Egypt was growing dramatically. Although the Brooke Hospital for Animals was doing a good job there, animal neglect was a

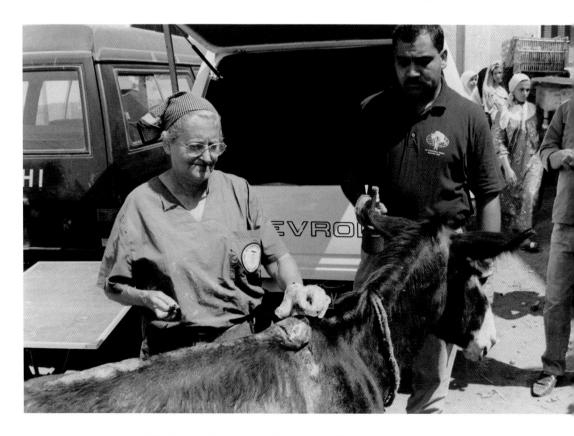

Working in Egypt with Dr Mourad Ragheb.

vast problem in that country and the donkeys needed our help. Andrew Trawford visited early in the year to look for premises halfway between Cairo and Alexandria so that we could expand our work in Egypt. We were devastated, therefore, when we learned that the Egyptian government had decided to privatise the country's veterinary services. Until then we had been working through this government department and the only way we could continue working there was to register the charity in Egypt. This would entail very long and complicated procedures which we were not in a position to undertake at that time. We decided that, sadly, the project would have to cease and, knowing it would be uneconomical to bring the mobile units back to the UK, we agreed to hand them over to the Brooke Hospital, specifying that they were to be used to help the donkeys in Egypt.

Visiting Ethiopia in 1986 I had been appalled to see the condition of both the people and donkeys, and I had immediately arranged for teams to visit regularly to treat as many donkeys as they could, with the co-operation of the Veterinary Faculty of Addis Ababa University in Debre

One of the vets working in Ethiopia.

Zeit. Dr Feseha Gebreab of the Faculty very kindly agreed to become our Project Leader, and since then mobile units had been set up and regular visits were made by our teams. I was happy in the knowledge that we could at least help some of the donkeys there and, by doing so, give valuable assistance to their impoverished owners.

Andrew travelled from Egypt to Ethiopia, where the mobile clinic continued to make inroads into the health and welfare of many donkeys. The work was concentrated in areas of large donkey populations, where the donkey was of vital importance to the economy. During the first month alone the clinic provided 1,169 treatments. The advantage of having the clinic run by staff from the local veterinary university meant that, apart from the regular treatment and care for the donkeys in the markets and villages, students could also go out with the clinic for training, so that when they left the university they could take their knowledge and interest in donkey welfare to other parts of Ethiopia.

In Mexico we were encouraged to learn that, at last, the government was beginning to show some interest in the dreadful market at San Bernabe, and had promised to fund improvements to provide better facilities. The two mobile clinics were visiting villages, markets and rubbish dumps and progress was being made, albeit slowly.

April

Establishing a third Centre for EST continually occupied my thoughts and I found myself increasingly drawn to the county of my birth – Yorkshire. I heard that my old home, Ash Grove, between Elland and Brighouse, was being developed, and I wondered if there might be a chance that we could build a Centre there. The director of the development company, Mr Cockroft, was an extremely pleasant man and he showed me all around the new development. It seemed very strange to walk into the bedroom where I was born to find it had been divided up and that a kitchen unit stood in the exact spot where I made my entrance into the world! Sadly, however, the site proved to be unsuitable for various reasons: it was on low land adjacent to the canal and a large power station had been built on the opposite bank. I really didn't feel it had the right atmosphere for a Centre, particularly in view of the large clouds of smoke emanating from the tall chimneys.

Feeling somewhat disappointed, I decided to visit Leeds City Council, where I was given a cordial reception by Mr Phillip Young of Leeds Leisure Services. I put forward my idea, and he promised to look out for any suitable buildings or land in the area.

May

During the winter the donkeys cannot go out in the fields, as their small, sharp hooves would cause the pasture to turn into a morass of mud, and there would be insufficient grass for the summer. So in the autumn they are all brought into large, airy wintering barns which have 'run-out' yards enabling them to walk around in the fresh air whenever they feel the need. Depending on weather conditions, the donkeys are let out into the fields again in the late spring, and the arrival of our Donkey Week visitors this year coincided with what we call 'turn-out'. At East Axnoller Farm, near Beaminster in Dorset, everyone stood and watched the donkeys as they trotted out of the big barn along the track to the fields. As soon as the donkeys saw the fresh spring grass they broke into a gallop, thundering around the fields, kicking up their legs and braying with excitement. It was the most wonderful sight.

Feeding our large family of donkeys and giving them the care and attention they need involves a great deal of fundraising. Administration costs are kept to a minimum, so that the donkeys receive the absolute maximum from funds raised. I have always felt that people who send us donations should be able to come and see how their money is being used without being charged for the privilege, so admission to the Donkey Sanctuary is free. Visitors who enjoy their time here will recommend our charity to friends and relatives who, in turn, may well become supporters themselves. The Sanctuary is open from 9am until dusk every day of the year so that people can visit whenever they wish, to see how happy and contented the donkeys are. We don't publish glossy brochures or magazines or organise fundraising dinners where a possible loss may be incurred. A large amount of our funds is kept in building societies and higher interest banking accounts, and are monitored weekly to gain the best interest rates. I don't like the charity to gamble on the Stock Market. Marie Wilson, our Legacy Officer, is kept very busy all through the year, as legacies are a major source of the charity's income. On receipt of a legacy the family of the deceased is always thanked and the name of their loved-one is placed on our Memory Wall at the Sanctuary.

One day I went into the Isolation Unit where the new arrivals are housed. It was heartbreaking to see, in the airy stable, four little donkeys, their heads held down and eyes fixed upon the ground. Their coats were matted and full of lice. One of them, Stephany, was so downcast she seemed to be cowering as she stood. I went in immediately, and

Turn-out at East Axnoller Farm.

she seemed to perk up a bit as I gave her a big cuddle. The manager appeared at the door and was really surprised that Stephany had let me near her. Apparently she hated any human contact. The four donkeys had been rescued from a dealer after being imported from Ireland and it was comforting to know that they could now look forward to a real donkey heaven with security for the rest of their lives.

Of course the high standard of care given to our donkeys often means that many of them live to a ripe old age. It is difficult to determine the age of a donkey accurately, but we had two donkeys at the Sanctuary, Arkle and Flash, who could boast over 100 years between them! *Country Life* magazine took a great interest in them and featured them in one of their issues. Arkle and Flash certainly enjoyed their retirement here, although they have both since died – Arkle in 1996 aged 52 and Flash in 2001 aged a magnificent 57!

June

I have always felt that some donkeys benefit from individual care and attention, and for this reason we run a fostering scheme, whereby selected donkeys are fostered to suitable homes, although still under the ownership of the Donkey Sanctuary. There are strict criteria: foster owners must have at least two donkeys. They are social animals and a donkey on its own would get very lonely. All homes are checked for suitability, and prospective owners are required to attend a training course on donkey management. Once in the home the donkeys are visited regularly by our dedicated welfare officers, and, in the unlikely event that problems arise, the donkeys will return to the Sanctuary.

Arkle and Flash.

In 1995 there were over 1,300 donkeys fostered in private homes, and Winston's story is a typical one. He was relinquished to the Sanctuary in 1981 from a home in Birmingham and, as he was such a loving little donkey, we decided to send him to a foster home with a friend named Pickle. Winston and Pickle stayed in the foster home for seven years until July 1990 when it was found that both donkeys were rather overweight and needed a more controlled grazing system. Unfortunately Pickle died in September of that year, and Winston was chosen to work at the Slade Centre, giving daily rides to children with special needs and disabilities. He got on famously with the children and was soon a favourite, but we recently found that Winston had rather sensitive feet, and because of this we felt he should retire. As luck would have it, the Welfare Department was seeking a donkey suitable for the fostering scheme to accompany Sadie, who was on her own and in need of a friend. Winston was suggested and, having been introduced, they became firm friends. I'm pleased to say that they settled in their new home very quickly and they're loving every minute!

Winston.

July

In 1993 the late Lord Houghton of Sowerby had proposed setting up a
'Dog Control and Welfare Council'. I had for a long time been concerned
that many animal welfare laws were hopelessly out of date, and
appalled at conditions for animals in pet shops – little birds from hot
countries crammed into cages in freezing temperatures, and rabbits in
cages too small for them. Anyone could open a pet shop without
suitable qualifications; all they had to do was promise to undertake a
training course in the future. I approached Lord Soulsby of Swaffham
Prior to discuss the possibility of setting up an advisory body on
companion animal welfare which would encompass Lord Houghton's
original suggestion. I have long been an admirer of Lawson Soulsby;
he is amazingly active and is chairman of many committees for both
human and animal welfare. The fact that he would be involved in setting
up a council for companion animal welfare would, I knew, ensure its
success.

   Lawson agreed that the idea was good, and he and I discussed how it
should be progressed. I was extremely keen to get this underway and
offered to act as Secretariat. In the first instance a steering committee
was organised and, in July, together with representatives from other
animal welfare organisations, I attended the first meeting in the House
of Lords. Everyone agreed that a council should be set up along the same
lines as the Farm Animal Welfare Council (FAWC) which was funded by
the government. Lord Soulsby discussed the proposal with members of
the government but, unfortunately, he was advised that no funds were
available. However, it was indicated that if the Companion Animal
Welfare Council (as it was to be known) was self-funding for a period of
three years and could produce reports which could be made available to
assist with future legislation, the government might well reconsider
taking over its work. As well as running the Secretariat, I immediately
agreed to undertake fundraising, and requests were sent to all companion
animal welfare charities for a three-year funding commitment, to which
most agreed. From then on regular meetings of the steering committee
were held to discuss the way forward.

August

I'm sure none of us will forget the nuclear disaster at Chernobyl in the
Ukraine in 1986, the effects of which caused suffering to hundreds of

people for many miles around the area, and are still doing so. A charity named Chernobyl Children Lifeline was helping children from neighbouring Belarus to forget their problems for a while by bringing them to the UK to stay with families here and provide interesting entertainment for them. The charity wrote to us, asking if the children could spend a day at the Slade Centre, where they could meet the donkeys and join in the activities. Of course we were pleased to oblige and since then the visits have become a regular event for different groups of children from the same area. Although they cannot speak English, an interpreter accompanies them, and both they and the staff really enjoy their visits.

September
Press and media interest in the Donkey Sanctuary had been steadily

The Playdays van.

increasing over the years. There were various articles and features in the local and national press and we were regularly visited by television companies. The programme makers from the BBC series 'Playdays' arrived with the presenter bringing along a brightly patterned van and the puppets Peggy Patch and the Why Bird. This provided some extra interest for our visitors at the time. West Country Television had also used the Sanctuary to film some of their 'Birthday' series. The programme consisted of five-minute slots between main programmes every day for a week, with the presenter at different venues within the Sanctuary.

October

A story in our newly-published *Donkey Tales* attracted the interest of a local radio station and was then picked up by press and television companies around the world! I had (perhaps unwisely!) mentioned in the book that donkeys, especially those owned by publicans, could easily learn to enjoy alcohol, from which they had to be gradually weaned on arrival at the Sanctuary. I was amazed to receive requests for interviews from many radio and television stations in the UK, as well as from the USA, Canada, South Africa and Ireland – the phone didn't stop ringing for at least two weeks!

Talking of donkeys and publicans, I was delighted to meet Mr Splane of Corky's Pub in Stoke-on-Trent, who was so interested in donkeys and their welfare that he kept a collecting box in his pub, and held events to raise funds for the Sanctuary. He decided to adopt one of our donkeys on his visit, but couldn't decide which one – so he ended up adopting all eight!

The next CEBEC meeting was held at the RSPCA Centre in King's Lynn. The Centre was built specifically to look after marine life when disaster struck, particularly seals and the birds that suffer as a result of oil spillages. I was pleased to be able to tell our host, Peter Davies, Director General of the RSPCA, how impressed I was with the Centre.

I was delighted when Alexandra Bastedo, star of the 1960s cult series 'The Champions', rang to say she would like to come and see our donkeys. She had just published her first book, *Beware Dobermans, Donkeys and Ducks*, and she sent me a copy. We obviously shared the same passion for donkeys – Alexandra had turned her home into an animal sanctuary with, at that time, around 100 animals, including dogs, donkeys, cats and chipmunks. It was hard to imagine that this very elegant lady was equally at home while mixing with celebrities or scrubbing out stables!

One day, the postman brought a strange parcel. He handed it to me, pointing out the unpleasant smell and, on removing the brown paper sealed with sellotape, I found a large sausage! Examining the label I was horrified to see that this was made with donkey meat. I immediately realised that this could be proof that donkeys were being transported from Eastern Europe to be slaughtered for the meat market, as I was not aware of anywhere in Western Europe where donkeys were being bred for this purpose. I hastily put it in the freezer and, on my next visit to London, I called at the offices of the *Mail on Sunday* to show the sausage to Roderick Gilchrist, the Deputy Editor. He passed me on to one of his reporters, who interviewed me and took photographs of the sausage but, unfortunately, they didn't print the story. I

Donkey meat sausage.

was so disappointed, as I felt this would have made the public aware of the suffering caused to equines by transporting them across Europe for slaughter in an inhumane manner.

Brian Bagwell, Deputy Administrator since 1981, had been feeling increasingly unwell during the year, and eventually under doctor's orders he had to take a long sick leave. I missed him badly; he dealt with the farms and building projects, and we had discussed the progress of the Sanctuary and future projects daily. His ill health eventually led to his retirement, which was announced at Memorial Day. Filling his place would be difficult, but the Trustees agreed that Mal Squance, who had been at the Sanctuary since 1981, would be of immense value as my deputy, as she was very knowledgeable in all aspects of the Sanctuary's work. Mal has the amazing knack of being able to study documents and pick out the important aspects immediately, and this has enabled her to formalise much of the charity's documentation over the years. She copes with a staggering amount of work, overseeing the Welfare Department, the Irish Sanctuary, Overseas, Fundraising, the main office and staff, as well as the administration of EST and the setting up of the trading company! How she does it I'll never know – she's an excellent 'right hand'.

I try to arrange a meeting of all members of staff at least once a year and the best time to get everyone together is before the marquee is dismantled following Memorial Day. I have always regarded the staff as members of a large family but, particularly on the outlying farms, it is not easy to keep everyone up to date with the work we are doing both in the UK and overseas. I feel that everyone should be given the opportunity to get together to be advised of the latest developments by the executives and managers. It is also an opportunity to renew old friendships and introduce new members of staff. As many as possible attend, leaving a skeleton staff on each farm to look after the donkeys, and I think this annual meeting is essential to ensure the smooth running of the Sanctuary.

November

To promote donkeys and the Donkey Sanctuary I attend various veterinary lectures and symposia throughout the world and I was invited to attend a meeting in Cambridge focussing on equine research. Research can be a very contentious issue and many students at veterinary universities are becoming less willing to become involved with intrusive research. On this occasion the main theme of the meeting was to ensure that ongoing research projects were not overlapping, so that intrusive programmes were not duplicated unnecessarily. The meeting was held in a large ground floor room with big windows at one end, and halfway through the meeting students started throwing buckets of water at the windows to protest against intrusive research. The curtains were swiftly drawn and the meeting continued, but I felt very uncomfortable to learn of research being undertaken that I couldn't possibly condone, and it renewed my resolve that the Donkey Sanctuary would never be a part of any such programme.

The production of our Newsletters and other printed material has always been a major part of our work. I have always rejected any suggestions that we should produce glossy publications, as the high costs involved would reduce the amount of money we can spend on the donkeys' welfare. However our list of subscribers was growing daily, and printing the Newsletter was now a massive operation which had totally outgrown the small printing room at Slade House Farm. We decided, therefore, that a large barn at Brookfield Farm, approximately three miles from Slade House Farm, should be converted for this purpose. This was successfully achieved and, with plenty of storage space for the vast quantities of paper required and the addition of new printing machines, we were able to continue printing the Newsletters in the same tried and tested way at minimal cost.

December

By the end of the year we felt we were winning on Grand Turk! All the donkeys had been rounded up and Michael Crane, accompanied by Andrew, June and Dawn Butt, a veterinary nurse, had visited to treat the unfit ones and castrate some of the stallions. However, there were far too many donkeys on the island and we had to think of a solution to the problem. Andrew Trawford had spent many years in Jamaica as a member of the Government Veterinary Service and, after a great deal of discussion with the government, it was agreed that some donkeys could be taken to a place called Paradise Park in Jamaica. The Park would set up a breeding programme to produce larger, stronger donkeys, which could be 'loaned' to local farmers. Donkeys were still used by farmers to carry sugar cane and coffee beans in from the hills during the harvesting season, but there was a shortage of suitable donkeys and those from Grand Turk would be ideal. The best way to transport the donkeys was by air, and we were surprised at how well the donkeys coped with the flight. The sixteen chosen donkeys were loaded into containers which were lifted onto the aircraft and none of them suffered any ill effects from the journey.

Financial difficulties hit many charities during the year for a variety of reasons, mainly thought to be as a result of enthusiasm for having a go on the National Lottery, which commenced in November 1994. This seemed to affect the smaller charities, and they were often not able to weather the storm. On several occasions we had to take donkeys into care from organisations less fortunate than ourselves and I was content in the knowledge that the Donkey Sanctuary remained in a position where my resolve that no donkey would ever be refused admittance could continue.

1 9 9 6

FIRE AT THE
DONKEY SANCTUARY

January

Friday the 19th January is a date I will remember with nightmares for years. At around 10.30pm I was woken from a deep sleep by the phone at my bedside. The Sanctuary fire alarm is an automated service that rings and plays a recorded message in the event of an emergency. On hearing the words 'There is a fire at the Donkey Sanctuary' I leapt out of bed, threw on my clothes and in the freezing night air I rushed across the lane that separates my home from the Sanctuary. I could see immediately that the eight-bay New Barn was on fire (see previous page for picture). The night watchman had already phoned the fire service, and was now trying to control the fire with an extinguisher, but it was immediately obvious that the barn was well alight – and inside were eighty elderly donkeys. John Pile, one of the farm managers, arrived on the scene and the three of us quickly ran around and opened the doors leading to the paddocks. Most of the donkeys trotted out quite happily, although some seemed reluctant to leave the ever-increasing warmth of the barn! With pushing and cajoling, however, we were able to get them all out, with our eyes and theirs blinded by the thick smoke.

We had a list of staff who could be called in an emergency, and John and I ran back into the office to call as many as we could. Staff would be needed to move the donkeys to a safer area – they were too close to the barn and we thought they might hamper the firemen's efforts to put out the fire. The list had been typed in normal sized print and our sore, streaming eyes made reading it very difficult. I made a mental note to ensure it was reproduced in large print for the future! Three fire engines arrived, and so did seventeen of our staff. Burning bales of hay and straw were dragged into the main yard and the main structure of the barn was hosed down. The bales were still smouldering, and it was obvious that the firemen would have to stay for some time to make sure the fire was completely out. Bless them, they joined us in moving the donkeys up to the Slade Centre, the only place we could think of that was dry and warm and where they could spend a comfortable night. It was quite a long way for some of the very elderly donkeys and a 'guard of honour' was formed, through which the donkeys passed – some trotting with excitement and the very old ones walking at a much more sedate pace.

We think the cause of the fire was a cigarette end, possibly tossed thoughtlessly into the barn by a visitor, where it had smouldered for some time before catching the straw alight. Thanks to our vigilant night watchman, a disaster had been narrowly averted. Subsequent checks by our veterinary staff established that the donkeys had not suffered any damage and were in fine fettle – probably better than some of the staff who, without any breathing equipment, had inhaled quite a lot of smoke.

In early January I went to London for a CEBEC meeting to be held at the offices of Radcliffe, Crossman, Block, a firm of solicitors, just across the road from the Houses of Parliament. Having arrived early, I had some time to spare, so I slipped into St Margaret's Church in the grounds of Westminster Abbey. It was warm and peaceful, and my eye was soon caught by a beautifully illuminated nativity scene near the altar. I gazed entranced at it, but immediately realised that the most important animal was missing – there was no donkey! I couldn't believe it; it just didn't seem right that, after fighting for its recognition by society all around the world, I should discover the donkey was left out of this tableau. I approached the only person who appeared to be in authority at that time of the morning – a gentleman quietly sweeping the aisles. 'Excuse me,' I said, 'can you tell me why there is no donkey in your Nativity scene?' He looked at me rather pitifully, leaned on his brush and said seriously, ''Cos the camels are too big.' 'The camels are too big?' I asked. 'Yes,' came the reply, 'you see, when Epiphany arrives, the Kings come in, and what with the camels being so big we have to take the donkey out – he was there at Christmas though.' I went to the meeting musing on the many reasons why donkeys lose out, but over-large camels was definitely a new one on me!

While I was in London a very sick donkey came into the Sanctuary. Her name was Cabbage, and she was in what the vets described as a very poor state. Cabbage had been put into foal many times, and it was possible she was in foal again, as she had been running with stallions who had bullied her. She was blind in the left eye and deaf in the left ear, probably due to a blow to the head, and she had to be led to food and water. She also had a terrible abscess on her left shoulder which needed a great deal of treatment before it was persuaded to heal. Cabbage and her friend Tammie took up residence in the main yard at Slade House Farm. Also in the main yard was the farm managers' office, in what was the old dairy. John Pile and John Rabjohns, the farm managers at the time, had turned the dairy into a nice working office. The Sanctuary has a team of gardeners, led by Tim Mason, who specialises in flowers and plants for herbal remedies. From one plant,

Tim had managed to divide and grow a few aloe vera plants, which are reputed to have a high nutritional value. He was persuaded, somewhat reluctantly, to give one of these tender plants to John Pile to help make the office look more homely. The plant stood on a shelf over a warm radiator and for months John cared for it, watering it lovingly, until one day he decided to move it onto his desk. It looked really good, and he set off to find Tim to come and see the results of his hard work. You wouldn't believe that a half blind, half deaf donkey, who still had to be led to food, would even consider pushing a door open to go into the office – and even less, that she would find the most tasty fresh meal she had ever consumed – but she did! John arrived with Tim to be greeted by a backside sticking out of the door, and when Cabbage turned to face him, a piece of the plant was disappearing into her mouth, brown juice running down her muzzle. John said he could swear she was smiling. She seemed to perk up after eating the plant, which was more than could be said of John and Tim!

Cabbage with the remains of the aloe vera plant.

February

This month once again brought disaster at Villanueva de la Vera. A positive response had been received from our meetings with the mayor and the villagers who had promised to protect the donkey. Misty was used again this year and, unfortunately, the villagers were outnumbered by a large group of drunken youths who punched and kicked to the ground those people trying to protect the donkey. For two and a half hours he was dragged through the cobbled streets and he fell more than thirty times. After the event all the hair on his hind quarters and the top of his tail had been pulled off, leaving bare skin. All we could do was to dress his wounds and leave him to recover quietly from his horrific ordeal. We decided there and then to launch another petition, aiming to collect a million signatures to present personally to the Spanish Ambassador in London the following January.

I had been thinking that some new blood on the Trustee board would be useful, and in Professor Stuart Reid I found the ideal candidate. I'd first met Stuart when he was studying for his PhD at the University of Glasgow, and the Donkey Sanctuary had funded his research on sarcoids. His work had an impact not only on donkeys but a spin-off helped cancer research as well. They found that the papillomavirus partially responsible for the sarcoid was related to that found in cervical cancer in women. Stuart's work was so important that he was soon offered a Professorship, and he became the youngest to reach this high academic status. In addition to his veterinary research skills, Stuart is also very 'computer literate'. He has assisted our charities in many ways over the years; he arranged for a team from the IT department to visit the Glasgow Veterinary School to see how their computer programme worked, and was instrumental in introducing the Sanctuary to the Internet, arranging, in the early stages, for our web pages to be channelled through Glasgow University's internet site. I was proud to introduce Stuart to the Trustees, who all agreed that this highly regarded young man would be of immense value to the team, and that he should join the board at the Trustees meeting in June.

March

I frequently mention beach donkeys in our Newsletters; they are the only working donkeys in the UK and I feel that, provided they are fit and well cared-for, they provide a wonderful service to children and provide happy memories of donkeys as the children grow older. Our

Welfare Officers regularly check donkeys working on the beaches during the summer season, but it was easy to lose track of them during the winter months.

We were contacted by the owner of the Barmouth beach donkeys as, despite support from us, a planning application to build a winter shelter for the donkeys on his land had been refused. This meant they had no respite from the inclement weather in their exposed field and they seemed destined to have a very hard winter indeed. We offered to take them into our care but the owner was very fond of them and didn't want to lose them. There seemed to be only one answer. To keep the donkeys dry and warm until accommodation could be found we loaned warm, waterproof rugs.

The puppet show in Mexico.

April

When June returned from her visit to Mexico with John Sharples, Director of the International League for the Protection of Horses (ILPH), I was interested to hear of an ingenious method of teaching donkey care developed by two of our Mexican staff. After the competitions for the best kept donkey and horse, which June and John judged, Dr Aline de Aluja and the staff held a puppet show. The puppets portrayed two donkeys and two owners (one good, kind owner and one bad, cruel owner). Of course the good owner was the hero at the end of the day. It was a hilarious show and the children and adults really loved it. At the end of the show the puppets asked the children questions on the correct treatment of donkeys and horses. The first one to shout out the right answer received a prize.

I regularly attend meetings of the All Party Animal Welfare Group which are held in the House of Commons. The group includes members of both Houses of Parliament and animal welfare organisations. I was very pleased to be asked to speak at one of these meetings on the problems we had encountered at the annual fiesta in Villanueva de la Vera. I was given a very sympathetic hearing and ended by saying that it seemed we were fighting a small war in favour of the donkey. To my surprise, Tony Banks MP jumped up, saying, 'I have one complaint with regard to Dr Svendsen's talk. It's that I don't think it should be a small war – it should be a large one!' and he sat down to a round of applause.

The RSPCA acts as a link between the committee of Eurogroup for Animal Welfare and animal welfare societies in the UK, including the Donkey Sanctuary. I attended a consultative meeting during which the group's director, David Wilkins, gave a report on activities in Europe, and this gave me a very good opportunity to point out the problems of the Spanish fiesta. Mr Wilkins very kindly offered to make arrangements for me to speak at a meeting of the Intergroup on the Welfare and Conservation of Animals in Strasbourg, which consisted of MEPs with a particular interest in animal welfare. We received a wonderful response from many MEPs, who agreed to meet me and give support at the meeting.

May

Philip Young of Leeds Leisure Services invited me to Leeds to look at three possible sites for our new EST Centre, and when I visited in May he took me to see them all. The first two sites were unsuitable for various reasons but we then went to see some buildings owned by the council which they believed might be converted for the new EST Centre. Stank Hall Barn was on the outskirts of Leeds and was obviously a property of great historical interest, comprising a main barn, several smaller barns and outbuildings, with a small paddock alongside. I had my doubts as to its suitability, but a site meeting was held and the proposals were put to the planning authority. In the event the property was considered to be unsuitable, which, looking back now, was just as well. The conversion costs would have been enormous and I don't think it would ever have been the ideal place. Everyone at the council understood the problems, and they continued to search for a suitable site.

Mozart was a rather elderly donkey, just over 25 years old, who had lived with the same family for 23 years. As too often happens, his owners gradually became too elderly to look after him, and for the last two and a half years he had simply been left shut in a stable which was never mucked out, and he was only occasionally given some hay. When the owner's wife died, the husband found it difficult even to visit the stable, and Mozart rarely had food or, even worse, water. The husband then died, and their daughter contacted us, as she felt she could not cope.

With great difficulty, for Mozart was terrified of humans, he was coaxed into our specially adapted donkey lorry and taken a short distance to our nearest holding base. Our Welfare Officer, Shelagh Steel, was horrified on his arrival. His feet were twisted and overgrown from standing on the deep filthy floor, and he was crawling with lice. Mozart was gently led into a stable, where he immediately went into a corner, cowering with fear when Shelagh tried to get near him. After the first day, during which he was able to get over the journey, Shelagh let down the bars of the stable, but Mozart was too frightened to come out. Gradually over the next few days he became a little braver, so Shelagh tried putting him in a field with a very gentle, elderly donkey, but Mozart was so terrified that he ran away! He was extremely emotionally disturbed. Slowly, however, he began to improve and was transferred to the Sanctuary. I nearly cried on his arrival, but with time he became much braver and began to venture out into the paddock, even playing with one of the special balls we provide for the donkeys' amusement! These are called 'horse balls' and they look like small 'space hoppers'. The donkeys can pick them up with their teeth and throw them – occasionally surprising an unsuspecting visitor who might be passing

Mozart.

by. He also made two friends, Sootie and Minor, both single donkeys who had lost their partners. He became much more approachable, although the member of staff caring for him did comment to me, 'He can be a bit handy with his back legs'! Veterinary examinations showed that he had a heart murmur but despite this he settled down to enjoy his life at the Sanctuary.

June

Prince Sadruddin Aga Khan* is the Founder and President of The Bellerive Foundation, the aims of which are to foster the protection of the environment, the conservation of nature and natural resources and respect for all life. We received an offer of land in Greece which could be used for caring for donkeys, but unfortunately we'd had to turn this down as our funds were committed elsewhere. Prince Sadruddin and his wife, Princess Catherine, were keen to build a donkey shelter on the island of Patmos, and they asked if I would visit to give my advice. The Prince and his wife, who is a Patron of Patmos Animal Lovers, are delightful people and are totally dedicated to animal welfare. In Greece donkeys are still worked very hard. There is little education on how to look after them and, as a consequence, a great deal of unnecessary suffering is caused. There have also been stories that when donkeys become too old to work they are turned loose to fend for themselves or, even worse, pushed over cliffs to be killed by the rocks beneath.

The site for the shelter was ideal. It had all the necessary facilities, a level area for grazing, and to the rear there was a fairly steep hill, where I knew the donkeys would enjoy exercising and browsing. We promised to return to Patmos if we were needed, and looked forward to seeing how the project progressed.

We were pleased to welcome a large contingent from the Dutch Donkey Breed Society. They were fascinated by their visit to the Sanctuary and impressed with all the facilities we had, including, of course, our donkey hospital. Shortly afterwards a Dutch television company came to film the Sanctuary and, judging by the large number of letters, phone calls and donations received, the programme was obviously well received.

I was making regular visits to Scotland, particularly to the University of Glasgow, where the building of the Weipers Centre was progressing

* Sadly, Prince Sadruddin Aga Khan passed away in May 2003.

well. I was delighted to see that the donkey boxes, funded by IDPT, were already occupied by donkeys receiving special veterinary treatment. On this occasion I was invited to the annual Senate dinner – a very great honour. Tradition is upheld throughout the university and everyone there is proud of its reputation, the high quality of its professors and the achievements of its students.

A very sad occasion was the death of little Gretal. Hansel and Gretal were amongst my first rescues in 1974. When the two little donkeys came in they were in such a terrible state that neither the vets nor I thought they had any chance of survival. However, after 20 happy years with us, Hansel had died in January 1994; Gretal had been allowed to stay with Hansel's body for at least an hour after his death, as we know from experience that this helps a donkey to accept that its companion has gone, otherwise it can spend days constantly looking for its friend and can pine even to the point of death. Sadly Gretal died on 20th June. It doesn't seem to matter how many donkeys we have; each one is an individual and it really hurt me to lose Gretal.

Following reports of sidewinder missiles being fired from the backs of donkeys in Afghanistan we were appalled to hear that rebels used a donkey packed with 130lb of dynamite to launch an attack on a police station in rural Colombia, in which eleven officers were killed. A National Police spokesman said that the so-called 'burro bomb' was detonated by remote control when the donkey sauntered up to within feet of police headquarters in Chalan, an isolated town in the mountainous northern Sucre province. This type of cruelty must surely be abhorrent to everyone.

July

We are always searching for good homes for our young, fit donkeys and, although the conditions we set are strict for the sake of the donkeys' welfare, they can benefit enormously from individual care and attention from their foster owners. I was touched to receive a letter from a couple, who took another of our foster donkeys into their home as a replacement for Jason, who had sadly died:

'We would like to thank you for the arrival of Stanley and thought that you would be pleased to hear how well he has settled into his new home and befriended our dear Sally. Stanley is a beautiful donkey, very affectionate and,

as you mentioned, a wonderful character. He has certainly lifted the grey cloud hanging over us all since the sad death of dear Jason. Sally was so excited when Stanley arrived and within a couple of days they were starting to build up a friendship which under the circumstances we felt would take more time. Sally and Stanley are already playing together at regular intervals and Stanley seems very happy in his new surroundings. He has fitted in so well with all our other pets, in particular with Willie, our ram, who really believes that he is a donkey, even down to queuing for the farrier! Obviously we are very pleased and relieved as we did wonder how Willie would react. He was absolutely devoted to dear Jason and never left his side, even at the end.

'Although we are delighted with Stanley as part of our family, dear Jason will never be forgotten. He will always be part of us here. We would be so grateful if you would mention Jason, Sally and Stanley's arrival in a forthcoming Newsletter. We feel that it may help others when faced with similar circumstances, to understand that something good can come out of a tragic happening. Stanley has certainly managed to give us all a new lease of life over the past few weeks.'

August

Wonderful news doesn't come all that often, but we were delighted to be given permission to build a clinic in Ethiopia, in the grounds of the Faculty of Veterinary Medicine of Addis Ababa University in Debre Zeit. Believe it or not, at just the right time a magnificent donation was offered to us by a couple who had supported the Donkey Sanctuary for many years and who had, in the past, been wonderful foster parents to four of our donkeys. The couple had, however, now moved abroad and the donkeys had been returned to the Sanctuary. The donation was to be used specifically for the building of the clinic. So in September Andrew and June went to Ethiopia on a twofold mission, firstly to look at the site and discuss the building plans, and secondly, to assess the possibility of expanding our work to other parts of the country, particularly in the north. By doing this we could help donkeys not only in and around Debre Zeit but we could also bring help to literally thousands of other donkeys in Ethiopia.

The sixteen donkeys that flew from Grand Turk to Jamaica at the beginning of the year were all doing well in their new lush pastures, very different to the scrub land they were used to. Despite this, and our successful castration programme, there were still problems with the donkeys in the compound on Grand Turk. The local children had

The donkeys from Grand Turk enjoying their new home in Jamaica.

eagerly helped with the rounding up of the donkeys, for which they received a small reward and, unfortunately, this proved to be the undoing of the project! Having run free for so many years the donkeys didn't like being restricted, and they quickly managed to break down the fences and escape. Once again the local children rounded them up; although the fencing was improved the donkeys still got out. It finally sank in that the children were going back to the compound after the adults had gone home and were letting the donkeys out, so that they could have the fun of rounding them up again and receive another reward! We decided to move more donkeys to Jamaica before the end of the year if possible, as we felt this would leave those remaining on Grand Turk adequate grazing. Water was laid on in the compound, which would be left open for the donkeys to enter, and we hoped that this arrangement would mean they would no longer be a nuisance to the people in the town. Several of the mares in Jamaica had already produced 'cubbies', the Jamaican term for foals, and the loaning programme to local farmers was going well. Andrew arranged for colleagues to check the donkeys in Jamaica regularly to ensure their well-being, as well as monitoring the project himself from time to time.

September

It seems unbelievable that the suffering endured by Mozart, the donkey, could happen somewhere else – but it did. Like Mozart, Barnaby had experienced a terrible life. He spent seven months of each year tethered in a small pen in a dark shed. He was beaten and left without water for days at a time. Unfortunately, his rescuer was unable to re-home him as, understandably, Barnaby had developed quite a nasty streak and tended to bite the hand that fed him! Barnaby settled down well at the Sanctuary and, once among donkey friends, his behaviour improved enormously.

October

Back in 1989 Steve Springford became one of the first Trustees of The Elisabeth Svendsen Trust for Children and Donkeys. Steve had been involved with the Donkey Sanctuary for many years before that and, as a director of a video production company, he had produced one of our early videos. He became a loyal supporter, raising funds by running stalls at EST Festivals. He is now a director of Celador Productions, which produces television programmes such as 'The National Lottery - Winning Lines' and 'Who Wants to be a Millionaire' - you'll see his name on the credits at the end of these programmes. He has also worked with many famous names, including Cliff Richard and Jasper Carrott, and is the proud owner of his own donkeys.

As was the case with Stuart Reid, I knew that Steve would be a very useful member of the board of Trustees of the Donkey Sanctuary, particularly in view of his knowledge and expertise in the media industry. It was agreed he would attend his first Trustees meeting in December.

December

Late in 1996 we heard of the death of Derek Tangye, the well known author of the *Minack Chronicles* and loving owner of two donkeys, Merlin and Susie. Before his death, Mr Tangye had requested that donations in lieu of flowers at his funeral should be given to the Donkey Sanctuary, which we were grateful to receive. Merlin and Susie came into our care and a close eye was kept on them as they were obviously stressed, having lost their loving owner. At the time there was a possibility that they might eventually go back into the care of the new tenant at Mr

Merlin and Susie.

Tangye's cottage in Penzance under our foster scheme, but in the event this didn't prove possible. In the meantime they were very popular with our visitors, especially those who knew of the donkeys' background. The two donkeys remained close friends, and I was amused to hear from one of our staff that he had been watching them as they strolled around our main yard. All of a sudden Merlin decided he wanted to go into the barn. He got halfway across the yard and looked back – Susie wasn't following! So he went back, took hold of her collar and tried to pull her along! They knew they were celebrities, and they regularly posed for the cameras.

We also gained two additional members of staff at the end of the year. I had really missed Paul since he left the Sanctuary's employment in 1994 to set up a video company and gain more business experience. He had always shared my love of donkeys, and had worked his way up the Sanctuary ladder. I was delighted when, at the end of the year, he agreed to return as joint Deputy Administrator to work alongside Mal. I knew he would strengthen our administrative team enormously. In addition, John Carroll was selected to join the Sanctuary as Finance Director, having previously worked with a large national charity. He proved a very able member of our team, not only being an excellent accountant but having the experience of working for a charity and with good links to the Charity Commission.

1 9 9 7
GOOD NEWS FOR BUTCH
BUT BAD NEWS FOR ME!

January

Delivery of the petition for our campaign to bring attention to the dreadful treatment of the donkey in the annual Fiesta in Villanueva de la Vera was planned for 30th January. The previous day donkeys and carts were taken to London from our Birmingham EST Centre in our specially adapted lorry. I was so proud to see the donkeys on that beautiful but cold morning – they looked so smart and were ready for the excitement of the day ahead. Katie Boyle and Virginia McKenna agreed to join us, sitting in the carts as we made our way around Belgrave Square to the Spanish Embassy. I was delighted to see that many of our supporters had turned up to add weight to our campaign and, under police guidance, we arrived at the door of the Embassy. We were told that the Ambassador was not available, but the Agricultural Counsellor, Dr Rafael Cavestany, came to see us, showing great interest in our campaign and accepting our petition of over a quarter of a million signatures. He spent some time talking to us, and we crossed our fingers that our campaign would persuade the Spanish authorities to make some big changes in Villanueva de la Vera.

The petition against the fiesta in Villanueva was delivered to the Spanish Embassy (above) after a donkey-drawn parade around Belgrave Square (left).

I was invited to give a lecture to the delegates at the annual Congress of the Association of Veterinary Students in Bristol. I feel it is important to bring donkey welfare to the attention of veterinary students, as education of young people is paramount in ensuring that future generations are aware of the donkey's needs. The enthusiasm of students is always very rewarding, and it's amazing how many of them apply to 'see practice' at our donkey hospital. At the end of the lecture each student was given a copy of the Sanctuary's reference book, *The Professional Handbook of the Donkey*, which I'm sure they will find useful once they are 'out in the field'.

February

My lecture in Bristol was immediately followed by a visit to Leeds to see a piece of land which the council could make available to us in Eccup. I was really excited when I saw the beautiful area, surrounded by fields and with a lovely pine forest at the rear of the proposed site. It was approximately eight miles north of Leeds, and adjacent to Lineham Farm Children's Charity. This organisation gives children from the city the wonderful opportunity to enjoy country life for a while. It is run as a small farm, and the children are set tasks to look after the various animals in residence, and are able to enjoy both the indoor and outdoor facilities. On my first visit I was pleased to meet Councillor Denise Atkinson, a former Lord Mayor of Leeds and one of the founders of Lineham Farm, and Maggie Warwick, Head of the Centre. I knew instinctively that this was the right place for our third EST Centre, and the two ladies offered to give us all the help they could. Arrangements were put in hand for Trustees and Executives to see the site and without exception they agreed with me. Our surveyor, Mark Thomson, immediately submitted the planning application for a Centre to be built on similar lines to the one in Sutton Park. He negotiated the terms of the lease and sent out tenders for the building work.

March

I am always so grateful to our supporters who send donations and raise funds for our charities, and I was even more delighted to learn that some of our staff had decided to undertake a sponsored parachute jump to raise funds for our overseas projects to celebrate the 21st anniversary of the IDPT. Catherine Morriss, Canny Harris, Sharon McConnell and Sue Lark did a short training course before jumping out of a plane over Dunkeswell airfield. I was told later that Sharon had caused some alarm; she was the first to jump, and the others couldn't see her as they parachuted to the ground – apparently Sharon was so light that, on leaving the plane, she had floated upwards first! However they all landed safely and their dare-devil antics raised over £1,000 for the charity. Malcolm Salter, manager of Brookfield Farm, also raised funds for the Sanctuary. A keen cross-country runner, he took part in the London Marathon and very kindly presented us with the marvellous sum of £750.

April

The contract with our practice vets, Ikin and Oxenham, terminated in April and it was agreed that Michael Crane would become a direct employee of the Donkey Sanctuary. At the same time we welcomed David Montiel from Mexico. We felt that bringing some of the vets from our overseas projects to spend periods of time at the Sanctuary would help them gain knowledge and expertise on donkey welfare with our veterinary team. I knew that the knowledge David would gain during his time with us would be of enormous benefit to the donkeys in Mexico.

David quickly became a familiar face around the Sanctuary and was very popular with the staff.

The Elisabeth Svendsen Trust for Children and Donkeys had been established as a separate charity in 1989 because the objectives of the Slade Centre restricted the work with donkeys and special needs children to a 25-mile radius of Sidmouth. The objectives of both charities were similar and I had become concerned that the work involved and the administration costs of running two separate charities were unnecessarily high. For this reason, and following discussions with the Trustees of both charities, I asked the Charity Commission if the Slade Centre could be absorbed into EST. The Commission understood the problems and it was agreed that the two charities would become one at the end of the financial year.

May

The fifteenth Donkey Week took place in May and, once again, it was very well attended. Selected accommodation in Sidmouth and the surrounding area, from hotels and guest houses to caravan parks and self-catering bungalows, is available. All the proprietors in our scheme donate 10% of our Donkey Weekers' accommodation costs to the Sanctuary. The journey to Sidmouth is made as easy as possible. Members of staff greet the visitors at Exeter train and coach stations, helping with luggage and guiding everyone onto the coaches which transport them to their accommodation. Daily trips are arranged to our outlying farms, which are not usually open to visitors. Each farm has different qualities, with delightful walks and extra little 'events' laid on.

Earlier in the year George Greenshields Sculptures had offered to produce a life-sized bronze donkey for us and, following discussions on how this could best be utilised, the Administrators agreed to adapt the rear garden at Slade House Farm to provide a quiet area with plaques and benches which could be dedicated by supporters to the memory of their loved-ones. The sculpture would be the centrepiece. The sculptor, Ray Gonzales, needed a model, which had to be a perfectly proportioned donkey – and we chose Russell, who at that time was working at the Slade Centre. A few months later, it was exciting to watch as this splendid sculpture was put in place in the centre of what has since become known as the Russell Memorial Garden. A moving opening ceremony was held during Donkey Week,

Opening the Russell Memorial Garden.

and the first memorial plaque set in amongst the heathers was dedicated to Derek and Jeannie Tangye.

June

Although all donkeys need care, it can get very difficult for the older ones. They can live to more than 50 years of age and they suffer from very similar complaints as many OAPs! Arthritis can be even more painful when four legs are involved, and our geriatrics find getting up in the morning very difficult. We used to use peat under their bedding to give them a good hoof grip, but we felt that the use of so much peat was not environmentally friendly. After various trials we found that deep straw, sometimes with shavings underneath, provided an alternative.

July

The age of a donkey is assessed by its teeth, and this is pretty accurate up to about twenty years old. After that, it becomes more difficult, as the wear is affected by feeding habits during its life; the top teeth can wear down to the gums while the lower teeth slope out at an ever-increasing angle. Eating becomes difficult and can be painful, as the back teeth tend to become sharp and pointed. Special feed is needed to keep these geriatrics in good health and our experts at the Sanctuary have devised diets for the very elderly. By 50 years of age special mashes and grated carrots are sometimes all some donkeys can manage. By that age you would think they would be very quiet and docile, but you should see them if another donkey comes near their feed bucket!

August

A German television film crew came to visit and we walked through the main yard, where all the donkeys were standing peacefully, enjoying the sun on their backs. 'Why do they stand so quietly?' asked one of the crew, 'Why aren't they all trotting around?' I explained that most of the donkeys were between 40 and 50 years of age and it wasn't usual for elderly people in retirement homes to be constantly on the move.

In September I was given the opportunity to present a paper at the 16th International Conference of the World Association for the Advancement of Veterinary Parasitology (WAAVP) in Sun City, South Africa. These conferences give us a great opportunity to spread our message on donkey welfare to veterinarians from all around the world, and the subject for my paper was 'Improving the equine by parasitic control'. I was also invited to participate in two of the ancilliary workshops at the conference, and give a five-minute talk in each.

I would describe Sun City as a small Las Vegas, with enormous gambling machines in almost every hotel. The lecture suite comprised a large theatre which could accommodate up to 1,500 delegates, around which were a number of smaller rooms allocated to the various lectures and workshops. I was enormously relieved when my lecture was successfully completed, and I decided to visit the room where Dr Aline de Aluja was talking on pigs and the conditions in which they were reared in Mexico. As I entered the room there was a young man sitting on the floor, his face a peculiar shade of green and yellow. Concerned as to his health, I asked him what the problem was. He explained that he, along with his fellow students from the University of South Africa, had volunteered to operate the video machines and slide projectors for the conference lectures, and he had been chosen to work the machine for Dr Aline. 'Of all the jobs I've done,' he said, 'and I've even watched vivisections in the university – these are the worst pictures I've ever seen! I don't think I can do this job much longer!' I must say I understood what he meant when I went into the room – Aline was happily showing slides which showed in great detail how pigs in many villages in Mexico were fed on human waste collected from open latrines!

September

The death of Diana, Princess of Wales, at the end of August affected everyone. There was an air of sadness throughout the Sanctuary – even the donkeys seemed quieter than usual to those visitors and staff who were at the Sanctuary on the day of her funeral in early September. Many people sent us donations in memory of Princess Diana, and we decided to build a small memorial opposite the entrance to the Slade Centre, where people could sit quietly if they wished. It's a lovely tranquil area, with an ornamental fountain and benches set in a small garden, partially enclosed with trelliswork and climbing shrubs.

It was rapidly becoming apparent that, with the increasing expansion of the Donkey Sanctuary, not only was more land needed, but more office space as well. We were very fortunate when the ideal opportunity arose to buy Trow Farm, situated right next door to Slade House Farm. Being so close meant that equipment and facilities could be shared and,

Princess Diana memorial garden.

as there was no need for a live-in manager, some of the buildings could be converted for use as offices. There was a great deal of work to be done on the farm to make it suitable for donkeys, but there was plenty of grazing land, and we all felt it was going to be of great benefit to the Sanctuary. Completion of the purchase took place in September.

October

Work to set up the Companion Animal Welfare Council was progressing and in early October I went up to London to meet with Sir Colin Spedding, Chairman of the Farm Animal Welfare Council and advisor to CAWC, Peter Davies of the RSPCA, and Professor Andrew Higgins, Chief Executive of the Animal Health Trust, to discuss the financial implications of the Council. We met at the Blue Cross Animal Hospital situated just behind Victoria Coach Station. The meeting had been arranged for 8am, so that I would have plenty of time to return to Devon afterwards for an afternoon meeting. I was able to produce a financial statement of what funds I anticipated raising from animal welfare organisations and a three-year budget plan was soon established.

The meeting was finished by 9.15am and, dragging my case containing my overnight things, I left the others, and set off to find a taxi to take me to Waterloo Station. My train was due to leave in thirty minutes. As I walked I kept glancing backwards trying to hail a taxi. Suddenly I fell into a hole left by council workmen who had removed some trees that had been set within the pavement. Although the hole had been filled with gravel, this had sunk down, leaving a square about 8" deep. I was badly shaken and, when I tried to move, I felt a sharp pain in my right ankle which had come to rest in a very awkward position. Passers-by were very helpful. One gentleman, whose office was close by, sat with me until the ambulance arrived. My ankle was put in a brightly coloured splint and off we went to St Thomas's Hospital, arriving at about 10 o'clock.

Although I realised I would not be returning to Devon quite as soon as planned, I wasn't prepared for the long day ahead! I was taken to the Accident and Emergency Department and it was almost an hour before a nurse came to assess my problem. She took one look at my ankle and, strapping it up again, she apologised and said I would have to wait, as they were having a very busy day.

I was able to contact Mal at the office, and she arranged that Paul would come up from Devon to collect me, once my ankle had been dealt with. In the waiting room I passed the time chatting to a young man on one side of me who thought he'd broken his toe, and a rather irritable businessman on the other side who constantly looked at his watch and complained about the long wait he was experiencing. Eventually, at 12.30pm I was sent for an X-ray, after which the radiologist vaguely told me that I would just have to wait to find out if my ankle was broken. Back in the A & E department I was given a bed in a cubicle, which was a great relief for my throbbing ankle, and I rested there quietly listening to everything happening around me. I felt full of admiration for the sister in charge, who dealt calmly and efficiently with the many aspects of her work in the department. Her job was not made any easier by constant complaints from the businessman, who kept appearing from the waiting room, growing more irritable by the minute, and taking little notice when being told that he would just have to wait. While I waited two paramedics came in with an elderly gentleman on their trolley, who appeared to be unconscious. He looked rather scruffy and unclean and I immediately noticed that a rather unpleasant smell was pervading the room. The sister grimaced and backed away, saying to the paramedics, 'For goodness' sake, don't bring him in here – he's just very drunk!' They answered, 'We had no alternative, so where shall we put him?' 'Put him in cubicle 5,' said the sister, already searching for some fresh-air spray.

It wasn't until the middle of the afternoon that the doctor came to tell me that my ankle was broken, and I would be allowed to go home once it had been plastered. While waiting, I heard the doctor explaining to the young man in the adjacent cubicle that his X-ray had confirmed a broken toe and, after a conversation with the sister, a face appeared round the curtain, and in a dejected voice the young man told me, 'I've been here all day, and now I've been told I'm not being plastered, and to put my shoe on and go home! I don't know why I bothered!'

The sister had called the Social Services and the two people who arrived were immediately pointed towards the dreadful smell in cubicle 5. Loading the still comatose old man back onto a trolley, they wheeled him away. The nurse was complaining to me that the cubicle couldn't be used again until it was fumigated, when the businessman appeared, very angry by now and threatening to complain to his MP. A sudden smile came over the sister's face. 'Don't worry,' she said to him, 'we now have cubicle 5 ready for you'!

I was eventually 'plastered' at 7 o'clock in the evening, by which time Paul had arrived to take me home. I looked in horror at the new car he'd just bought – it was a tiny Ford Ka, but, propped up with cushions kindly sent by June, it was a surprisingly comfortable journey despite my throbbing ankle. What a day!

Unfortunately I had to miss Memorial Day, but I managed to write a poem to be read out during the Service, entitled 'From a Donkey'.

We've had our sad and weary days
As we've stumbled along the lane
We've felt a stick across our back
Overburdened and often in pain.
For countless hours on the scorching sand
We've carried our precious loads
For many years we've had no rest
Forced on by sticks and goads.
When winter came, with the snow and rain
We've shivered in the cold
No warmth, no food awarded us
Our bones ached as we grew old.
But oh! One blessed glorious day
He looked down on us from above
Our wounds and sores were clear to see
He knew we needed love.
And so today we've found our rest
We've found our donkey heaven
We're fed and loved in peaceful quiet
In a wonderful corner of Devon.

(With apologies to all good beach donkey operators!)

Although I was using crutches, I managed to get up to London later that month to attend a CAWC steering committee meeting. By now the committee was finalising the framework to ensure the independence of the council. A charitable trust, The Welfare Fund for Companion Animals, was to hold the contributions from the animal welfare organisations and would pass these funds to the council as and when required. It was agreed that Trustees for this new organisation should be sought from the Royal Society of Veterinary Surgeons, the Law Society and the Institute of Chartered Accountants, and the Presidents of these bodies were asked to put forward the names of their members who might be willing and able to serve as Trustees. It was also decided that members of the Council would be chosen by a completely independent Appointments Committee. Lawson Soulsby secured the agreement of four prominent people to undertake this role – Sir James Armour, Sir David Williams, Sir Christopher Payne and Baroness Mallalieu. Also present at the meeting was Mr Michael Harbottle, a solicitor who had been recommended to assist with the setting up of the Charitable Trust and the Council.

November

I have mentioned in an earlier book the story of Butch (for a picture of Butch, see page 85). Butch and his elderly owner, Jack, had been inseparable for years, but eventually ill health forced Jack to send him into the Sanctuary. Jack was so fond of his friend that he travelled in our lorry from Leicester to be with Butch on the journey. Jack visited the Sanctuary regularly, and would sit for hours on a bench in the main yard with Butch's head on his shoulder. As Jack became more and more frail his family brought him, and on a couple of occasions we were able to collect him from his home so that he and Butch could be together. Sadly Jack died in October 1995, and Butch was still missing him desperately, despite being given extra love and attention from the staff.

Going out into the main yard on my crutches, I was surprised to see Butch standing quite still with his head on the shoulder of an elderly gentlemen sitting on one of the benches. As I hobbled across to the man he smiled at me and said, 'This is wonderful! This old donkey just came across and put his head on my shoulder and we've been here for nearly an hour!' I looked at Butch and could see that he was happy at last. Perhaps he thought the elderly man, with his grey hair, was Jack. The answer came to me in an instant – we would advertise in our local paper for a grey-haired 'donkey sitter'! Several offers were received, and a retired infant school teacher named Derek Bevan, who lived with his wife in nearby Budleigh Salterton took up the challenge! Butch took an instant shine to Mr Bevan, who twice a week drove to the Sanctuary to sit quietly with Butch's head resting on his shoulder. Mr Bevan said 'Butch is a wonderful old character and seems to perk up when I come to see him. He trots over and goes through the routine of putting his head on me. It's very touching, and I'm enjoying myself enormously.' At last – a happy Butch!

For many years I have been a member and Vice-President of Colaton Raleigh and District Ploughing Association, a local agricultural society. I was honoured this year by being promoted to President, and I offered

The donkey ploughing team.

the association the opportunity to hold their annual Produce Show and Ploughing Match at the Sanctuary. Our large marquee was filled to capacity with over 300 entries to the produce classes, including home-made cakes, jams, chutneys, vegetables, flower arrangements and artwork by children from local schools. A team of donkeys gave a wonderful demonstration of ploughing, which was much admired by fellow competitors who had brought along their horse teams. To encourage our staff, we arranged with the organiser for a special competition to find our best ploughman. The Donkey Sanctuary awarded a cup and a bottle of champagne for the winner. Of course there was a great deal of rivalry amongst the staff from the farms, and this year Rob Haywood, our manager at Town Barton farm, won the cup. It was a great pleasure to present the awards and it really was a most enjoyable day.

Last year I was delighted when Paul's daughter, Dawn, joined our staff. Dawn had, quite literally, grown up with donkeys and had spent most of her school holidays working as a groom in the main yard. However, she was now working as an office junior and trainee computer clerk, and I was thrilled to see the enthusiasm she put into her work. It was lovely to have three generations of Svendsens at the Sanctuary!

Under Paddy Barrett's watchful eye the Irish Sanctuary was going from strength to strength, with frequent visits from Mal Squance and Sarah Bagwell to ensure smooth running and support. There had been a terrible case during the year when an owner left 21 donkeys on a one-acre site with no grass or water. When the donkeys came into the Irish Sanctuary they were in such a terrible state, emaciated and dehydrated, that every one had to be put on a drip by the vet. One young foal sadly died, but we saved the rest, and three of the mares had since given birth to healthy foals. The owner was successfully prosecuted and given the option of a £10,000 fine or a £500 fine plus 6 months' imprisonment. He chose the latter. A separate case in Ireland on donkey cruelty resulted in the judge fining the defendant £700, adding that the money was to be paid to the Donkey Sanctuary!

I was very sad when June decided to resign as a Trustee of the Donkey Sanctuary. I suppose it was difficult as we had been close friends for such a long time, and she had become increasingly concerned about any conflicts of interest which might arise in her role as Trustee of the Donkey Sanctuary and an employee of IDPT.

December

I always try to take some leave over the Christmas and the New Year, when everything is much quieter from a business point of view. This year June and I decided to join the inaugural cruise of the P&O liner *Arcadia*. In charge of the ship was Captain Rory Smith and the itinerary included Gibraltar, Casablanca, Lanzarote, Tenerife and Madeira. On our first walk around the decks I was most surprised to hear a voice calling, 'Hello Dr S' – and there in front of us stood David Cook and his wife, Jill. They really are a lovely couple and they attend all our Donkey Weeks and fundraising events, running stalls to raise money for the donkeys. It was great to have them on board ship, and we were able to talk 'donkeys' to our hearts' content, becoming good friends into the bargain. We celebrated New Year's Eve by watching a spectacular firework display in Madeira, and together we all contemplated what was in store for the Donkey Sanctuary in the coming year.

1 9 9 8
INDIA – A NEW
OVERSEAS PROJECT

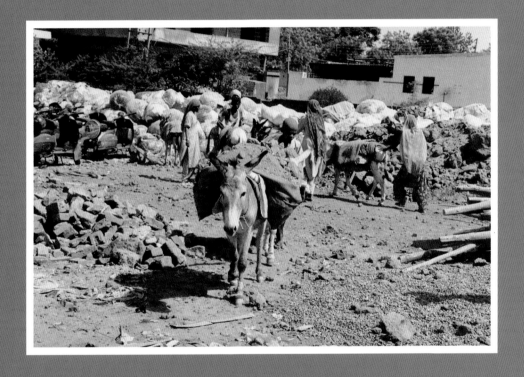

January

The year started with the most terrible storms and gales. What a winter we had! Fortunately all the donkeys at the Sanctuary had the opportunity to stay in their large airy barns in bad weather. During what we described as our 'hurricane day' (force 11 and gusting higher) the normal dignity of our elderly residents' perambulations around the yards was rudely shaken. Even when you weigh 160 kilos, a gust of wind from the rear can force you into a trot! The young donkeys seemed to love it, but the geriatrics decided discretion was the better part of valour and they stayed inside the barn. Having survived the wind, their dignity was even further shaken by their first steps into the now frosty yard – one slip and once again it was back into the barn.

June had read a report of an interview with Mrs Maneka Ghandi on the plight of animals in India, particularly donkeys. Mrs Ghandi was a minister in the Indian government, and ran an organisation called 'People for Animals'. June contacted her and Mrs Ghandi invited June to visit her to discuss the possibility of IDPT setting up a project there. A short time later I had the opportunity to meet Mrs Ghandi on one of her visits to London and was most impressed by her strength of character and determination to help animals in India. She was very hopeful we could work together.

On June's next trip to India she was accompanied by Andrew, and they were introduced to many people who could be useful in a new project. They visited different areas to establish where a project should be based, and their initial preference had been to start in Ahmedabad in Gujarat state. However, for various reasons, it was eventually agreed that, working through 'People for Animals', a site near Delhi would be easier to administer. Mrs Gandhi offered us part of her charity's compound outside Gurgaon in the village of Sadhrana, to use for our donkey project, and a small vehicle was purchased, which visited the building sites around Gurgaon and the brick kilns at Bhatti village. The working donkeys were in a terrible state, having to carry tremendously heavy loads of bricks over very tricky 'obstacle courses' to reach their destinations (see pictures opposite and on previous page).

One morning, during a meeting with John Carroll to discuss the financial implications of the Indian project, I was called to answer a phone call from Peter Feather, my nephew. My sister, Pat, had been rushed into intensive care at the Royal United Hospital in Bath, having

Working donkeys in India.

suffered a heart attack. I hurriedly packed a few clothes and drove to Bath as quickly as I could.

Although I was concerned to see that Pat was wired up to several machines, particularly a heart monitor, it was good to find that she was bright and cheerful. She explained that, luckily, the attack had occurred while she was in the car with Peter, having just arrived for dinner with her other son, Michael. The two of them had been able to rush Pat to a local hospital, where she was diagnosed and sent on to the Royal United. I sat with her until late in the evening, and promised that I would stay in Bath for the night so that I could visit her the next day. I managed to find accommodation for the night, but the hotel car park was full. I was just wondering what I should do when I spotted a small area of rough ground almost next to the hotel, and I felt the car would be safe there.

The following morning I returned to the hospital. Pat was still bright and cheerful as we chatted but, in the early afternoon, I saw to my horror that her heart monitor was changing from its steady rhythm and was registering a series of vertical zigzag lines – Pat was having another heart attack! I was asked to leave, and had a very long, anxious wait in the corridor before being advised that she was alright, although the doctor told me that she would have to have a pacemaker fitted without delay. I was told that I could return at around 8pm that evening.

The car park was full again when I returned to the hotel so I left my car on the rough ground. Returning to the car that evening, I was concerned to see that it was surrounded by some scruffy-looking people. I approached rather nervously but thankfully they were all very pleasant, and stepped back from the car. It appeared that I had parked in the place where the soup van usually stopped, and they were worried that they wouldn't get their supper!

Pat was able to have a pacemaker fitted the following morning and, fortunately, everything went well. Living on her own, Pat couldn't go back home immediately, so I was pleased to offer her the downstairs bedroom in my home for a couple of weeks to recuperate.

February

Patience is often badly needed in our job. Since 1981 we had been deeply concerned about donkeys that were being taken into the supposed care of an organisation in the Sussex area. At the time advertisements frequently appeared in the national press stating that, unless funds were received, the donkeys would be sent for slaughter. This continued despite all our offers to take the donkeys into our care. Following regular visits by our welfare officers (often meeting with a hostile reception) we had been able to take eleven donkeys into the Sanctuary in 1986. We thought our job was complete but, to our horror, the advertisements began appearing again, in a different area and under a different name! This time our welfare officers were not allowed access to monitor the donkeys, but we kept a close watch on the situation. However, in 1998 the owner of the organisation died, and at last the donkeys' dreams (and mine!) came true, when nine little donkeys – all with appallingly bad feet – came into the Sanctuary. It had taken nearly eighteen years to save these poor animals, but at last they were assured of a wonderful future being cared for and loved for the rest of their lives.

In principle we don't agree with buying donkeys at markets, because this can encourage greedy dealers to trade in a way we find abhorrent, but there are exceptions. Two of our supporters had seen two terrified little foals at a market. The foals were too young to have been parted from their mothers and were in a very frightened state. The concerned couple bought the foals, named them Tuppence and Midge, and contacted us. We immediately took the foals into our holding base near Buxton in Derbyshire. The same couple saw two more foals at the same market shortly afterwards, and bought them as well. All four foals were brought to Slade House Farm in our specially fitted lorry, and they settled together happily.

The couple who had purchased the foals asked if one of the last pair could be named Sabine, but they left it to us to name the second foal. A few weeks before they arrived I was touched to receive donations in memory of Mr Gail Gunderson, Vice-President of General Motors Europe, who had died suddenly in Switzerland. Mr Gunderson was a well known and popular man, and I was so grateful to his wife for choosing our charity to benefit at such a sad time. Mrs Gunderson asked if we could name a donkey 'Gail' in memory of her husband, so the arrival of the foals enabled us to grant her request. Little Gail was the weakest of the four foals, and had to be bottle fed at first, but gradually he grew strong and they were all much loved and admired by our many visitors.

We have always had close connections with Bicton Agricultural College, and members of our staff attend courses there on farm and pasture management, tractor driving, health and safety on the farm and other farm-related subjects. The college has a good reputation and I was delighted to be asked by its Principal, Malcolm Florey, to give a talk at a lunchtime meeting. I don't particularly like giving lunchtime lectures, as I worry throughout the meal and am afraid to have even a sip of wine! In this instance I was concerned about the content of my talk. The audience ranged from young students to highly professional lecturers, but all seemed to go well and I felt relaxed enough to relate an amusing (if not factually accurate!) tale from one of my journeys overseas:

June and I visited Ethiopia regularly, and the journey was always rather difficult. It's an overnight flight leaving Heathrow and arriving at around 6 o'clock the following morning. We then had to get straight down to work, despite the lack of sleep. June and I boarded the plane one evening wearing our Donkey Sanctuary uniforms in readiness for the work ahead, and we were instantly recognised by an immaculately dressed young air hostess. She said to me, 'You must be Dr Svendsen from the Donkey Sanctuary. I'm sure that, as a successful businesswoman yourself, you will be interested to know that all the crew members of this British Airways flight are women, including the pilot.' I agreed that this was indeed very interesting and during the flight June and I discussed how things had changed over the years. After a pleasant meal the young lady came and crouched down beside me and asked, 'Would you like to meet the Captain?' I said,'Yes, I'd love to – I'll follow you to the cockpit' She looked at me for a moment, and then said, 'Oh no, Dr Svendsen – we don't call it the cockpit on *this* flight!'

Villanueva de la Vera brought its usual problems, although the donkey was treated a little better this year – perhaps due to the intervention of Dr Rafael Cavestany, the Agricultural Counsellor at the Spanish

One of our donkeys at a Palm Sunday service.

Embassy, who had accepted our petition last year. We were now in the process of setting up an office in Spain, and had employed José Fernandez Gíl as a welfare officer. As a Spanish national, José might have more success in negotiations with the mayor of the village.

March

In contrast to the events at Villanueva de la Vera we had, for many years, received requests to take our donkeys to Palm Sunday services. Although they may look angelic, few donkeys at the Sanctuary can be trusted to behave themselves in church. However, with the co-operation of some members of staff and a conveniently placed bucket, we are able to help a few churches in the area on one of the most important events in the Christian calendar. We were honoured this year to receive an invitation to take a donkey along to the Palm Sunday service at Exeter Cathedral.

Dundas and Brandy were two donkeys determined to follow in Cabbage's footsteps. One morning a representative from an animal food company called and left some samples on John Pile's desk. Dundas was a very elderly donkey who usually had excellent manners, but he must have smelt the delicious aroma coming from the office and, with a little negotiation of the door clasp, he made his way in. As John told me later, it wouldn't have been so bad if Dundas had stuck to stealing the samples, but he was happily munching his way through John's computer print-out of donkeys' weights by the time he returned!

Not to be outdone, Brandy worked out how to get into the tack room at our Training Centre at Paccombe Farm. He doesn't mind demonstrating his achievement either – he pulls the latch down with his teeth, puts his little hoof around the door and pulls. No doubt he can smell the staff's biscuit supply!

April

In April I was joined at a presentation in the Queen's Hotel in Leeds by the EST Trustees and our Centre Principals to introduce our proposals to relevant education authority members and head teachers of special schools in the area. I welcomed the guests with an introductory talk on our work, Julie Courtney and Sue Brennan then spoke of the achievements of our Sidmouth and Birmingham Centres, and we had a lovely commendation from Mr Steve White, the head teacher of Bridge School, whose pupils regularly attended EST Birmingham. I was greatly encouraged by the interest shown, and

Ten-year Donkey Weekers in 1998.

could sense that working for children with special needs in Leeds was the right thing to do.

May

'The best ever Donkey Week' was the most repeated comment after our 16th event in May. From a total of 342 supporters who attended this year, 63 had attended for a total of 10 years or more. It really was fun and we were blessed with lovely weather. The donkeys had a huge audience for 'turn-out' and they made up for the winter months in their barns by galloping around the field and doing frequent victory rolls! Never had so many donkeys been groomed with such love!

June

A Trustees' meeting was held in June. The Trustees are kept fully informed of what is happening within the charity and, although regular updates are sent to them by letter, there is always a huge amount of paper work which has to be brought together. The meetings, sometimes held over two days, are long and intensive. Unfortunately, this particular meeting brought disappointment, as Johnny Morgan, one of our long-serving Trustees, had decided to retire from the board although, with his experience in banking, he was still prepared to give advice on a consultancy basis. I had recently met Wendy Manfield, who was Corporate Manager of Barclays Bank in Exeter and had been impressed by her warm, pleasant manner and obvious expertise. I instinctively knew that she would be an ideal Trustee. In the first instance the Trustees met Wendy on a social level, after which they were unanimous in agreeing that she should be invited to join the board.

The increasing number of visitors to the Sanctuary, plus two minor accidents and several near misses, had highlighted the problems of access to the Sanctuary. Vision in both directions at the junction with the main road was severely restricted, and we were worried that one day a more serious accident might occur. In 1993 initial discussions took place with the local council, and five years later the work began to replace the existing lane at its junction with the A3052 with a new junction approximately 80 metres from the original. The work was completed and opened to traffic on 9th June. To commemorate completion of the lane a tree was planted by Councillor Rod Ruffle, Chairman of Devon County Council's Environment Committee, and Councillor Stuart Hughes, local County Councillor and Chairman of the East Devon Highways Sub-Committee. The lane was flanked by 'Devon banks', on which John Rabjohns and his staff planted hundreds of daffodil bulbs, which give a wonderful display of colour each spring.

I was able to arrange a meeting with the Mexican Ambassador, Senor Santiago Onate, to see if he could use his influence to persuade the owners of San Bernabe market to improve the conditions there. There had been no progress despite our offers of help, and the ramps we had provided to unload the donkeys and horses had been discarded, as they were proving too difficult and time-consuming to move into place. As a result the animals continued to suffer the most appalling injuries when jumping out of the lorries. Senor Onate was very sympathetic but I'm afraid I was not convinced that he would be able to influence any major changes.

We were, however, able to expand our work in Mexico with a third mobile unit in the State of Tlaxcala. Again this was in conjunction with the ILPH, and there was no doubt that the condition of the equines we were now treating had improved enormously. Dr Aline de Aluja reported that there were 4,000 equines in 17 communities in the State

Our mobile unit at work in Mexico.

of Tlaxcala, and the teams would need anthelmintic (worming paste) for 21,000 animals in their care throughout Mexico.

July

I was delighted to perform the opening ceremony for a new building at our holding base in Derbyshire, comprising stables on the ground floor with a training centre above. Newton Farm, near Buxton, is a typically northern farm, set in the beautiful Peak District, with mainly stone buildings and dry stone walls surrounding many of the fields. We had been fortunate to acquire the farm in 1990 as a result of a successful application to the executors dealing with the estate of the late Mr Newton. Mr Newton had left instructions in his will that the farm was to be given to the charity that could best use it for animal welfare – and the Donkey Sanctuary was the lucky applicant! I knew it would be really useful as a resting base for donkeys being transported from Scotland and the north of England, as it is such a long journey to Devon. Donkeys in a poor condition would be able to stay there until we felt they were fit enough to cope with travelling to Devon. Although it was called Bull I'th Thorn Farm at that time, we changed the name in recognition of Mr Newton's generosity.

Ray Mutter and Julie Hussen had been employed at the Donkey Sanctuary in Sidmouth for many years. I knew they were going out together and I could see that they would be the ideal couple to run Newton Farm. I suggested it to them, and also hinted that it would be much better if they were married. I'm glad to say my little cupid's arrow struck home! It was lovely to see them on my visit – they were really happy together and were running the farm extremely well. The delicious food laid on for guests at the opening ceremony was provided by Madeline Newton, who is one of our regular Donkey Week visitors and who goes to see the donkeys at Newton Farm quite often, as she lives nearby. It was a thoroughly enjoyable day.

Work on the building of the clinic in Ethiopia had been progressing, albeit painfully slowly, but we hoped to be ready for an official opening in October. Unfortunately I was told that the vital equipment needed for the clinic – including the operating table, anaesthesia and surgical equipment – was stuck in a queue of cargo waiting to be flown to Debre Zeit; the waiting list was almost six months. Frantic negotiations were to no avail, and the opening of the clinic had to be re-scheduled.

I was encouraged, however, by the fact that the book I wrote in 1996, *Dusty, the Little Ethiopian Donkey* had, with the help of Dr Feseha, been translated into Amharic and was now being distributed to schools in many parts of Ethiopia. I was sure this would help in the children's education, although I understand that the staff and students at the University of Addis Ababa were also keen to read it! I was touched a couple of years later to hear from a lady named Kate Fereday, Founder of the Kindu Trust, a UK-based charity that provides and runs shelters for homeless children in Ethiopia. She sent us a copy of the Trust's newsletter which included a lovely picture of the children in Riggs House, Debark, having the 'Dusty' story read to them.

Following the success of this book I had also written *Joe, the Donkey who Flew to Jamaica*. Now I was in the process of writing the third book in the series, *Pepe, the Donkey who Went to Market*, and this time, for each copy sold in the UK, we promised to send a free copy to an impoverished school in Mexico.

David Montiel had now spent twelve months at the Sanctuary and was due to return to Mexico in September. David was so popular with everyone that a 'leaving party' was held at a local country club. Like everyone else, I was sad that he was leaving, and I wrote this poem which was read out at the party:

You came, you saw, you conquered
The hearts and minds of us all
No-one could guess what an impact you'd make
When you arrived, so quiet and so tall!
Within a few days you were into the job
The vets breathed a sigh of relief
As you tackled your tasks with the greatest
* of skill*
Whilst the girls thought you were Omar
* Shariff!*
You've joined in the fun, and managed to
* grin*
Even when things didn't go our way
You're one of our team, and we wouldn't
* feel mean*
If you suddenly decided to stay.
But alas and alack, you've got to go back
And it's Mexico that is the winner
For the donkeys out there will be walking
* on air*
Getting fat with your help – not thinner
So adieu, adios, buenos tardes to you
We all hope that you do really well.
But one thing we know, when you go away
We're all going to miss you like hell!

David Montiel.

Dr Getachew Mulugetta from our Ethiopian project had joined the veterinary team in March, and Mourad Ragheb joined us after David's departure. Although we no longer had a project in Egypt, Mourad Ragheb's general contribution to donkey welfare continued. He was always willing to investigate complaints we received of neglected and ill-treated donkeys in specific areas of Egypt – and we were seriously hoping to return to work there one day. We therefore invited Mourad to the UK to spend twelve months in practice at the Donkey Sanctuary. I have always admired Mourad's skill and his genuine love for donkeys. He joined our team of vets and nurses who give daily care to the donkeys and also carry out non-intrusive research which is, of course, passed on to the veterinary profession in general. This helps not only donkeys in this country but also overseas, where we are working hard to improve the often terrible lot of the donkey.

August

Donkeys were still coming into our care with the most terribly overgrown hooves. These not only caused them constant pain but would probably have a detrimental effect on their welfare as they grew older. Problems with donkey's feet are quite common at the Sanctuary; due to wear and tear, the pedal bone sometimes descends through the hoof until it comes into contact with the ground. Once this has happened, there is nothing that can be done for the poor donkey; it causes such great pain and makes walking impossible so that the best course of action is to put the donkey down. Our vets had the brilliant idea of making special shoes, which fit over the bottom of the hoof. Although this is not a long-term solution, it does enable a donkey to enjoy a little more time of happy retirement.

Sometimes events that appear horrific turn out well, and this was the case with Benjamin! His owner saw him lying in a ditch at the end of his field, and thought he had died. He called the vet, who said he thought Benjamin had broken his leg, and that he should be put down. They called the local knackerman to collect the poor doomed donkey but Benjamin took one look at the approaching lorry and, with a great leap, he was up and galloping around the field. He had certainly fooled everyone, and it was at this point that his owner decided to send him in to the Sanctuary, where he was found to be in excellent health!

I received the most beautiful letter one day that brought tears to my eyes. It was from a visitor to the Sanctuary, and she wrote as follows:

'Another year passes, for some with regret, for others with relief, only too pleased to see it gone. Nevertheless each passing year seems always, not only to throw up its fair share of tragedy, but also some truly magical moments. Picture if you will a fine, warm, sunny East Devon day, a windless almost breathless day. The yard at the Sanctuary, although full of donkeys, has the air of quiet contentment. It's early, only a few visitors have arrived, maybe the staff and donkeys realise it's just the calm before the storm and are making the most of it.

'We sit on one of the benches, just looking, alone with our thoughts, the tranquillity of the moment belying the suffering that had gone before. Can these wonderful animals ever trust again, can they ever forgive their tormentors? You could forgive them if they could not. Cabbage breaks the stillness, and with an air of insatiable curiosity wanders nonchalantly over to a child in a buggy, gently placing her head on the child's shoulder as if whispering some long held secret in its ear. Child and donkey held this position for some considerable time. We watched ... the child's father watched from a distance, neither wishing to destroy the moment ... What would happen next?

'Obvious really. Cabbage's secret now safe, she did what all good friends do. She took half a step back, bent forward and placed an approving kiss on her new friend's cheek. Anthropomorphic? Maybe, but I'd like to think not. No audible sound was exchanged between the two – but communication – yes, I'm sure. I often wonder what the secret was, but it was never mine to tell. For a brief moment in time I was excluded. It was a moment of tenderness, affection and trust I did not ... could not understand. I could only feel the magic. It would appear that if you are very lucky, donkeys will show you unconditional love and trust, and seem to forgive without a second thought.'

September

We are always happy to take in 'referrals', donkeys who need specialist treatment when the owners' own local vets do not have the necessary facilities. Our donkey hospital is very specially equipped and our vets and nurses can provide the best possible care for sick donkeys. No charge is ever made as we do this for the donkeys. A donkey named Jason was referred to us. He had been castrated some time earlier but there had been problems, as severe scar tissue had broken down and frequent abscesses were causing him a lot of pain and distress. Jason was one of four donkeys owned by Brian and Susie Perkins and in order to reduce Jason's stress during the time of his operation, his companion Charlie came with him. The operation was difficult but successful, and our vet Alex Thiemann hoped for a good recovery.

However for days afterwards Jason would not eat or drink, and we all thought we were going to lose him. In desperation we rang Susie and without hesitation she caught a train from Sheffield, leaving her husband to care for their other two donkeys. By the time she arrived Jason was fading fast. He had not taken any food or water for ten days, despite being tempted with everything we could think of. Susie was a 'Donkey Weeker' and already knew us well. I was quite emotional when

I met her as, to our amazement, Jason perked up and started eating as soon as he saw Susie! We were so excited; we kept hugging each other and Jason! Susie took Jason for walks along the hedgerow, talking to him and pointing out the juicy shoots for him to eat. He recovered as if by magic and a week after Susie's arrival he was fit enough to go home.

I always like to spend as much time as I can with my family. I had been able to visit all of my children this year, and also helped Sarah buy a small Victorian house in Greenwich, which she absolutely loved. It's not often the family can get together all at one time, so I was delighted when they all came to Sidmouth in August, and I planned a party with lots of surprises in store!

In the woods at Paccombe Farm is a large pond with a hut alongside where June and I would go sometimes to sit and watch the wildlife all around us. I decided that we, as a family, could spend a day there, holding competitions and having a barbecue lunch. A marquee was erected close to the pond, to give some shelter if the weather wasn't good. Happily, it turned out to be an absolutely beautiful day. When we had gathered, I gave each member of the family clues for a treasure hunt, all centred around the pond. After they had all returned, exhausted

Family boat race on the pond.

... and the chefs ...

but happy, they found a small rubber dinghy for each family and a boat race took place. I was the Admiral, and sat in a dinghy in the middle of the pond, with June in another as official starter and timekeeper. Despite the difficult manoeuvres and the shrieks of laughter, no-one actually fell in. After the excitement, out came the barbecue units and the men were delegated to cook our lunch. Of course, the necessary cook's aprons and hats were provided. What fun it was to be altogether again, and everyone had a wonderful time.

October

With the growth of the Sanctuary had come the need for additional administration staff, and the offices at Slade House Farm were now extremely cramped. While we were in the process of building a new office block at Trow Farm, it was necessary to lease some office accommodation in Honiton, about seven miles away. Paul and his new PA, Emma Woodward, moved in, together with Dawn, Mark Thomson, Rob Nichols and Michael Viksna, who had recently been appointed as Health & Safety Adviser. This wasn't an ideal situation but it solved the problem until the new offices were ready.

I'd really missed having cats around since our last cat, Sheba, had died, so when I heard of some oriental blue kittens for sale, June and I set off to look at them. Mrs Gurini had two or three kittens for sale and I fell in love straight away with the runt of the family; she was half the size of the others – very skinny and looking like a little wizened monkey. I felt she would be lonely on her own, so, of course, I had to choose another kitten as well! I was able to assure Mrs Gurini that I was happy to take on the responsibility of nursing the sickly kitten, and so off we went with two new additions to the family. We decided to call the skinny kitten Monkey, and chose the name Ming for her little friend. They settled in remarkably well, considering they had to share us with toy poodles, Tinkerbell and Bubbles, and standard poodles, Winnie and Maisie, as well as June's little dachshund, Zara. The kittens kept everyone amused. They obviously didn't like being at floor level at all, and we had to get used to flying cats appearing from the tops of the cupboards and landing on the nearest unsuspecting victim.

Monkey and me.

Ming.

November

Our supporters had been so generous in sending us donations to buy rugs for the donkeys that we now had more than enough for all the donkeys in the Sanctuary for the rest of their lives! Charity Commission regulations on 'restricted funding' ensure that donations received for a specific purpose are only used for that purpose, and, as a result, we had substantial funds tied up in the 'rug fund' that could be put to better use elsewhere. We had to apply to the Charity Commission for permission to release some of the money from the fund, so that it could be used for other essential purposes, leaving sufficient in the fund for the costs of replacing, cleaning and repairing the rugs we already had. We also had to advise our supporters that no more rugs were needed. This, I knew, would cause disappointment, as being able to buy something specific for a donkey was obviously very popular.

At last planning approval was received for the Leeds EST Centre and in November, along with Pat who was representing the Trustees, I went up to Leeds, to perform the 'turning of the first sod', with Councillor Brian Walker, Leader of Leeds City Council, who had been so helpful to us. Amongst those present were Bob Hicks, representing the builders, Quarmby Construction Company Ltd, David Horton, the architect and, representing Leeds City Council, John Thorpe and Roger Henderson. Bob Hicks presented us with a lovely silver spade. We all ventured into the middle of the field for the ceremony – we didn't stay there very long, though, as it started to snow and we were absolutely frozen! Even Pat's enthusiasm to use the spade diminished very quickly. The job done, we adjourned to Lineham Farm where Maggie Warwick, bless her, had laid on hot coffee and cakes, which were very welcome. The silver spade hangs on a wall at the Centre as a memento of the day.

Applications for the post of Principal of the Centre were sought through the national press and I was delighted when I heard that my cousin's daughter, Debbie Coombes, was one of the short-listed

Trixie wearing her rug.

candidates. During the visit to my old family home I had met my cousin Derrick and his wife Betsy, who told me of their daughter's successful career at a special needs school in the Leeds area. She was in fact in line for promotion to head teacher. I thought then that she would make an ideal Principal for the Leeds Centre, although I knew that Derrick wouldn't be too keen on the idea, as her prospects were so good under the safety of the education authority. As an 'interested party' I wasn't involved in the interviewing process, but Debbie came through with flying colours and the interviewing panel all agreed she had the qualities needed for the job. It was decided that Debbie should commence her employment in January 1999 to help co-ordinate the work, arrange the internal fixtures and fittings for the Centre and liaise with special schools to ensure their continued interest. She also had to learn all she could about donkeys before the Centre opened.

I hadn't been feeling too well and, on the spur of the moment, I decided to take a short break cruising to the West Indies on the *Vistafjord*. The only stress I felt on board was whether or not I could win the shuttleboard competition, and on my return home I felt much better.

There was a pile of paperwork awaiting me at the office and I got straight down to work. I usually come into the office on Saturday mornings, as I'm able to get on without interruption. For many years Ron Smith, a member of our Information Centre staff, had been coming into work earlier than was necessary on a Saturday morning so that he could bring me a welcome cup of Bovril and tell me his latest funny story! I'd just finished telling him about a letter I'd received from Abdalla in Lamu telling me how delighted he was that the local people were now bringing their donkeys into the Lamu Sanctuary when they suspected they were ill, rather than, as in the past, bringing the donkey in when it was too sick to be helped. Ron stood listening quietly, and then said with a grin on his face, 'Have you heard about the Kenyan who opened a small business in Leeds? ' 'No,' I said. 'Well,' Ron went on, 'the refuse collector came into the shop and asked him, "Where's your bin?" The owner looked at him and said, "I bin to Nairobi." "No," said the refuse collector, "Where's your wheely bin?" Back came the answer, "I weally, weally bin to Nairobi!"'

Not to be outdone, I responded with my little joke about the three nuns who were sitting on a bench when a streaker ran past. Two nuns had a stroke but the third couldn't reach! It's good to start the day with a laugh!

December

From my earlier autobiographies you will know that all my life I have loved sailing on the Norfolk Broads. This year we had a very special Christmas with my family joining me on the Broads, albeit all on their own boats. I arranged a dinghy race on Barton Broad, not realising how cold it would be. Although I had great fun, standing in command as Admiral, armed with a whistle and a Blue Peter flag, it was a freezing cold job. On Christmas morning we opened our presents on Paul's yacht, followed by lunch at a small hotel close by. I rather alarmed everyone early on Boxing Day morning when I awoke to find the cabin filled with what I thought was smoke. I leapt out of bed, yelling 'fire!', only to find that the haze was caused by my warm breath in the −5° temperature of the cabin!

It had been a hard year, but I was happy that I was able to be with my family and that the Donkey Sanctuary remained in fine fettle.

1 9 9 9
A VETERINARY CLINIC IN ETHIOPIA AND A NEW CENTRE IN LEEDS

Rosie

Simon

Kelly

William D

January

Another New Year started – the last of the Millennium! It was bitterly cold and pitch dark as I went outside. I usually get up at 5.30am and, after eating a light cereal breakfast, I feed all the animals, and then go into the aviary to feed the birds and check them all. I am in the office very early awaiting the postman.

After the Newsletter is sent out to our supporters, we can receive up to 3,000 letters a day and I always sort through the post to pick out special envelopes that I feel I should open personally. This helps me keep a close eye on how each department is running. I'm not sure how it first started, but John Pile is always there to help, and during this time together I learn much of what is happening around the farms. Once sorted through, the sacks of mail are sent to the main office, where they are all opened and sent to the appropriate departments.

Paul usually rings me early to discuss any problems he may have, and Mal comes upstairs as soon as she arrives to update me on the work within her remit. John Carroll is next on the list. He takes from me any legacy cheques that have arrived in the post, and we discuss the Sanctuary's financial situation, particularly on a Monday morning when we check that the Sanctuary's investments are getting the best interest rates. Andrew Trawford is the morning's final routine visitor, and he tells me of the latest veterinary news from the hospital or problems with particular donkeys within the last twenty-four hours. Sadly, as our herd grows older he often has news of donkeys which have died or been put to sleep. Having spoken to all the executives I am usually able to start my daily 'rounds' to check all the donkeys.

I was very pleased to receive a visit from the director of Paignton Zoo, Peter Stevens. He had heard of our work and of our interest in preserving the Poitou breed of donkey. I was equally interested in his zoo, which had made such a good name for itself. He advised me of the improvements which had been made there and of his great interest in breeding endangered species. I was, of course, delighted to show him around the Sanctuary and I felt that at some time in the future we might be able to work together to save some of the almost extinct species of donkeys in the world.

I had been closely involved in planning the new clinic in Ethiopia, and had worked with Dr Feseha and Andrew to make sure that all the needs of the donkeys would be met, so it was a great disappointment to me when, due to my ongoing stomach problems, I was unable to attend

The clinic in Ethiopia.

the re-scheduled official opening in January. I was, though, able to make a video presentation which was shown on the day, and Andrew, June and, of course, our Ethiopian vets were honoured by the presence of the British Ambassador. I had no doubt that the clinic would make a tremendous improvement to the working life of the Ethiopian people, in which the donkey plays such a vital part.

February

At their February meeting the Trustees gave serious consideration to my suggestion to incorporate the IDPT within the Donkey Sanctuary. It was becoming increasingly difficult and expensive to keep the three charities running as separate entities in line with charity regulations, and I felt the administration work would be eased enormously if these two charities became one. The Trustees agreed, and it was decided to put the proposal to the Charity Commissioners to see if it met with their approval.

Paul was also concerned about the level of individual care we were being able to give to each donkey on our farms. The ratio of staff to donkeys was higher at Slade House Farm, due in part to the fact that this was the only farm open to the public, who took up a proportion of the staff's time, and partly because of the various special groups of donkeys living there. At their meeting in February the Trustees agreed that more grooms should be appointed for the other farms to a level of one member of staff to every sixty donkeys. This would ensure that each donkey would receive a higher standard of care, such as more regular grooming and 'picking out' of their feet, the debris which collects under the hoof which must be removed regularly to prevent abscesses and other foot problems. Although I agreed wholeheartedly with the decision to employ another thirteen members of staff, I knew more fundraising would be needed to achieve this. To this end the Trustees agreed that Paul should embark on a trial direct mailing campaign. This was something I'd not really been keen on doing before, and I was unsure of the reaction of our present subscribers. However, the 60,000 people who were approached in the trial had completed 'Lifestyle' questionnaires and had confirmed that they would be prepared to donate to an animal charity.

I was pleased to receive a letter from the Charity Commission advising me of a proposed visit to the Sanctuary by two of their Commissioners. While I had sought the advice of the Charity Commission several times over the years since I first founded the Donkey Sanctuary, there had been little personal contact. I welcomed this visit, feeling quite sure that they would be happy with what I saw as a well run, well respected charity. However, this appeared not to be the case, and I was most upset to learn of their concern at the fact that we had family members working within the charity, in particular members of my own family. The Commission had asked that one of our Trustees be present when their representatives visited, and I immediately asked *all* the Trustees of all three charities to attend, which they did, as well as the charities' solicitor. On the day of the visit, the Trustees and the Executives waited well past the allotted hour for our visitors and I was surprised when, looking out of my office window, I could see the reason why – there they were, in the main yard, talking to the donkeys! When they eventually came in, the Trustees were brilliant; they explained my feelings so well when pointing out that Paul had over fourteen years' experience with the charity, having worked his way up from the bottom to his current position, and my grand-daughter, Dawn, was fulfilling her job as a junior, with the same salary and conditions as other office workers. Being from such a small community, many of the staff were related and I'd always found them honest and loyal. Families worked happily together as a team and it created a happy and contented environment for the donkeys. Having listened to what we had to say, the Commissioners admitted that they were following up one or two minor complaints they had received regarding the Donkey Sanctuary but had not found anything amiss. This was a great relief all round and I am pleased to say that, since that day, the Charity Commission has been very supportive of our charity – it certainly gave me a few nightmares though.

For the second year running we were delighted to receive a magnificent award of IR£15,000 from Joe Walsh, the Minister for Food and Agriculture in Ireland for our Cork Sanctuary. The Ministry quoted 'The Liscarroll Donkey Sanctuary has experienced major growth since its inception and while it is sad to see so many animals in the poor and neglected conditions in which they arrive, it is fantastic to see the presence of such a facility in rural Ireland. Now open for 11 years, 1,500 donkeys have passed through its gates, where 14 people are employed full-time, with 12 part-time in the care of the animals and the administrative mountain involved.'

March

We were surprised to receive a phone call from a Dutch television company. They produced a programme called 'Geef Nooit Op', similar to 'Jim'll Fix It', and they came to the Sanctuary with a team of eight, including Lotte, a twelve-year-old girl whose wish it was to visit us. We were used to television crews visiting, and we planned to take Lotte around the various departments. However, the story was to be slightly different and not one I felt Jimmy Saville would have wanted to take part in! The producers presented their story-line in the form of a fairytale. It was about Lotte, a little girl who had lost all her money. In the story her uncle had disappeared and, having changed into a donkey, he had decided that the Donkey Sanctuary was the best place to live. When Lotte came to visit her uncle (the donkey) he produced the money. To our surprise the crew wanted to film a donkey defecating, and had to wait some time for this natural event to happen! Then to our horror, they all knelt on the ground and pushed Dutch guilders into the steaming heap! I'm pleased to report that the £100 donation the film company gave to the Sanctuary at the end of the day was not collected this way.

April

The vets this year were stretched to the limits by the arrival of a little donkey named Bobby. In all our experience we had never seen a donkey with so many sarcoids. These small cancerous growths are quite common in donkeys but Bobby's sarcoids were extensive. It is always difficult to decide when an animal no longer has any quality of life, and we are prepared to euthanase a donkey when we think that all quality has gone, but in this case Bobby was a very young donkey, only one year old, and we felt we had to do all we could to help him. So, for the first time, we used donkey chemotherapy. We decided that three doses would be given, with a good gap in between. We all prayed that he would get better. Eventually we managed to rid him of the growths, but then a real tragedy occurred. Being a stallion, like all the other entire donkeys, he had to be castrated before being able to mix with our resident herd. The vets frequently castrate stallions, but for some unknown reason Bobby died under the anaesthetic. Everyone was heartbroken. He had been such a brave little donkey throughout all his veterinary treatment. Possibly, though, it was meant to be; our experience with sarcoids is that they nearly always recur. It didn't make it any easier, though. However, we had to put the tragedy at the back of our minds when we had an attempted breakout by some of our residents.

Mal Squance was working late one evening when she heard the scuffling of hooves outside her office window. She looked up to see six donkeys thundering towards the road! How they managed to release the two donkey-proof bolts on the door from main yard we'll never know, but they had. Mal dropped her work and raced outside. Two donkeys had turned to the right but, in a true donkey manner, the other four donkeys had decided to split forces and they turned left! Mal desperately ran after them as they hurtled towards the main A3052, and managed to stop any overtaking cars by shouting and waving her arms. She was, however, appalled when one driver completely ignored her and shot past. Her rage turned to enormous relief, though, when the car swung across in front of the donkeys, blocking their progress, and John Pile leapt out, legs and arms akimbo! Fortunately he had been on a shopping expedition and was just returning when he saw a 'very puffed out Mal' (his expression!). Together they were able to bring the donkeys back to the main yard.

After all our hard work the Companion Animal Welfare Council was to be officially launched. At the end of April I went up to London accompanied by Sue Harland, John Carroll and Gerard Bain, our Financial Accountant, to attend the reception in the House of Commons which the council had organised in conjunction with Lord Soulsby. A council meeting was held in the House of Lords during the afternoon prior to the launch, and it was agreed that the first work studies to be undertaken would be:

1.   Identification and registration of companion animals.
2.   Setting standards and controls for rescue societies.
3.   The welfare of companion animals in health and social care institutions.
4.   The welfare of exotics – standards and controls.

After the meeting we adjourned to the Jubilee Room adjacent to Westminster Hall for the official launch, generously sponsored by Pedigree Masterfoods. Many MPs and members of the House of Lords were present, and they were all interested to learn of this new organisation which would be able to give advice on any new legislation relating to companion animals. Members of animal welfare organisations also attended. Most of these were contributing towards the funding for the council, but one or two were not and, after a brief chat, I was able to persuade one of them to agree to contribute as well! A short talk was given by Lord Williams of Mostyn, the minister in charge of the Home Office at the time, and we were all encouraged by his enthusiasm. We were aware, however, that there was still a long way to go before the government would be in a position to take over responsibility for the council.

Towards the end of April my sister Pat and I enjoyed a week's holiday on the Norfolk Broads, accompanied by Pat's son, Peter. It was a wonderful week, but on the last evening we were in for a shock. We had anchored our boat on a bank just outside South Walsham Broad and, having safely moored, Peter went to have a hot shower. Poor lad, he was really looking forward to it and had insisted on showering first that evening because all week, by the time Pat and I finished in the bathroom, he never had enough hot water! Pat was sitting quietly reading and I was in the aft of the boat feeding the moorhens. An elderly gentleman on the boat next to us was trying to manoeuvre an aerial into a position which would give a clear picture on the television. His wife was in the cabin and we could hear her shouting, 'That's better –

no, it's worse now!' I was just shooing away a swan which was trying to steal the moorhens' bread when I heard a shout and, looking across, I saw that the man had fallen and was now lying on the bank. I jumped off and ran to him. He looked very pale and I was horrified when he explained in a weak voice that he'd just had a heart bypass and was feeling really ill. He obviously needed immediate medical help, so I rushed back to the boat to get my mobile phone. On hearing the commotion Pat looked up from her book and asked what she could do. 'Take some blankets,' I said. 'See if you can make him more comfortable.' Just as I got through to the emergency services I heard a thud and a scream and, looking over the side of the boat, there was Pat flat out on the bank as well! She had jumped off the boat onto the uneven ground, and her ankle was now at a very peculiar angle. As you can imagine, my phone conversation was more complicated than I first envisaged! 'We need at least one ambulance, if not two, as we have a man who may have had a heart attack and, from where I'm sitting, it looks as though my sister has broken her ankle!'

I shouted for Peter to come and help, explaining what had happened. He appeared, shaking his head and muttering, 'I was only having a blooming shower – how could so much happen in such a short time?' Dressing quickly, he joined me in helping to make Pat more comfortable, while someone from one of the other boats attended to the other casualty. By this time it had started to rain, and umbrellas were hastily fetched to hold over them. We were very relieved to hear the sirens of the ambulances approach from South Walsham village. Unfortunately they couldn't get very close, and the paramedics had to manoeuvre the stretchers along a narrow ridge with steep banks on either side. The doctor came to see Pat first, confirming immediately that she had indeed broken her ankle. He insisted that she lift herself from the wet grass and onto a first aid box he had brought with him, 'so that she didn't get piles'! He then went to attend to the poor gentleman close by, and I noticed that he was immediately fitted with an oxygen mask. The paramedics quickly put Pat's leg in splints, carried her up the bank and along the ridge to the ambulance. Peter and I hurriedly returned to the boat and grabbed some clothes and a few things for Pat. I believe the second ambulance took the gentleman to a hospital in Norwich, but we never heard what happened to him, despite our enquiries later. Poor Pat! Her ankle was badly fractured and needed to be operated on.

It was by now almost 9pm and, as there was no way Peter and I could get back to the boat, we rang the boatyard, who arranged to bring it back to the yard at Acle Bridge. We found a motel near the hospital which had none of the little toiletries usually found in hotels and, as neither of us had brought even a bar of soap with us, it was not the most comfortable of nights. In the morning Peter was able to fetch his car and, while Pat was having her operation, we managed to find better accommodation at Oulton Broad, and have something to eat at last! We were able to visit Pat the next day. She was remarkably cheerful, although she was concerned about how she would manage at home, as her ankle would be in plaster for eight weeks. I assured her that she must stay with me and, having arranged for an ambulance, we brought her back a week later and established her in my downstairs bedroom. What a holiday!

May

Donkey Week was upon us immediately afterwards, and I really enjoyed meeting all our 'regulars' again. Many of our Donkey Weekers knew Pat well from her time as Principal of the Slade Centre, so she had plenty of visitors.

The Hayloft.

While the Sanctuary caters for thousands of donkeys every day, up to now, humans had to make do with machines for drinks and snacks. However, with so many visitors coming to Slade House Farm, we decided it was time to open a restaurant. Rather than use hard-earned charity funds, it was agreed that the restaurant would be run by an independent organisation on a contract basis. The successful applicants were James and Julie Hall who were already running a company called 'Posh Nosh'. A loft overlooking main yard and the sea was converted and I was asked to officially open 'The Hayloft' at a low-key ceremony in April. Shortly afterwards a more 'party-like' opening was held, complete with music provided by a local jazz band.

June

Two years after the volcanic eruption on Montserrat in the West Indies, we were asked to help the donkeys on the island and Andrew went to assess the situation. His report was quite surprising and not really what we had anticipated. It seems the donkeys that were abandoned when their owners fled to the north after the eruption were doing very well. They were browsing through people's gardens and enjoying the crops left unattended. As a result their condition was excellent. However, in the north, the donkeys found their supplies of food severely restricted, as the islanders had set up new homes on land formerly used for their grazing. The World Society for the Protection of Animals was doing excellent work on the island on behalf of the animals, but it seemed certain that a compound would have to be built there to protect and feed the donkeys. Donkey numbers would also have to be controlled until the situation returned to normal.

July

Thanks to a brilliant suggestion from a member of our staff, Carole Cole, we started a new project which involved taking donkeys to visit residential homes for the elderly in the East Devon area.

Rainbow was 26-years old and had been with us for over 15 years, spending his time giving rides to children with special needs at the Slade Centre. Unfortunately he'd had to retire from this work as he had developed foot problems. He obviously missed his work, and when the donkeys were selected for each day's riding, Rainbow would wait at the gate hoping to be chosen. We decided to see if he would like to become part of this new project – and what a success it was! Rainbow really enjoyed going into the residents' rooms and brought such

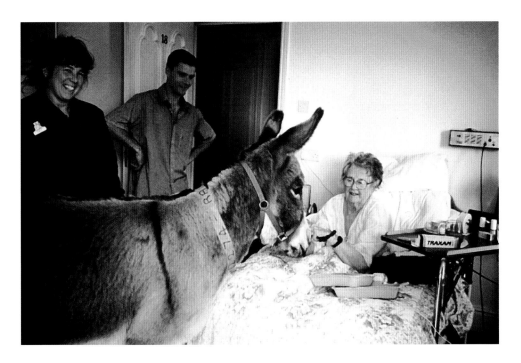

Rainbow on duty.

excitement and pleasure to many elderly people. In one particular case, two very elderly ladies, who spent their days in their own little worlds, never leaving their seats or taking part in any activities, suddenly became inspired by Rainbow's visit! They both stood up, took hold of the lead rein and walked off with Rainbow, closely followed by staff and carers, who had never seen these ladies so animated! The project, which at that time was known as 'Donkey Facilitated Therapy', was a great success and requests for donkey visits grew daily.

August
It was lovely to welcome Jean Gilchrist, Administrator of the KSPCA (Kenya Society for the Protection and Care of Animals), from Nairobi to the Sanctuary. Although a Scot, Jean had settled in Kenya and, being a dedicated animal lover, she was keen to help any animals found to be in trouble. Jean is particularly fond of donkeys and has been helping us since the early days of our work in Kenya. To help donkeys in areas that we don't reach, the IDPT awarded the KSPCA an annual grant to cover the costs of its 'donkey work'. This year, being aware that donkeys in northern Kenya needed help, we agreed to fund a vet employed by

the KSPCA to work in the north. During her visit to the Sanctuary, I was delighted to be able to repay some of the hospitality that Jean has always shown me and our teams when we visit Kenya.

This year the WAAVP Conference was held in Copenhagen and both Andrew and I were giving papers. With my daughter, Lise, and her family living in Denmark, I took the opportunity to visit them for a few days prior to the conference. Driving to Harwich to catch the ferry to Esberg, I couldn't help but notice the heavy traffic going in the opposite direction. It was the time of the solar eclipse and visitors were pouring into the West Country, where the best view in the UK was to be had. The sea was very rough on the ferry crossing and, although I managed to catch a glimpse of the eclipse in a very cloudy sky, a little girl standing close to me was overcome by seasickness – and I was in the direct line of fire! I decided that discretion was the better part of valour and returned swiftly to my cabin!

After seeing the family, it was lovely to be back in Copenhagen, which is a beautiful city. On the first evening the organisers arranged a dinner for the delegates in the glorious Town Hall, and the next night we were treated to a visit to the Tivoli Gardens, where Andrew and I shared a typical Danish-style dinner.

Sunday 22nd August was Festival day at the Sanctuary, held to raise funds for EST. The weather was fine but not too sunny (otherwise everyone would have vanished to the beach!) and over 15,000 people turned up! Julie Courtney and I were so grateful to those people who voluntarily ran stalls, gave entertainment, made music and generally helped out with all aspects of staging such a huge event. During the day, children who attended the Centre were presented with prizes – not always awarded for riding skills but for such important things as cheerfulness and courage. The prize-winners were so proud to receive their trophies and it was a very moving experience for all the spectators. My new book, *From Dawn to Dusk at the Donkey Sanctuary*, had just arrived from the publishers, and I spent the day autographing copies for those who had bought them. We sold over £2,000-worth of books and my wrists ached for days afterwards!

We were all shocked to hear the dreadful news that Gerald Hitchens, one of our lorry drivers, had died suddenly as a result of a heart attack. I was very fond of Gerald, who had often driven us to the airport during his years at the Sanctuary. Most of the staff attended his funeral and seeing the large numbers at the church in their Donkey Sanctuary uniforms brought a lump to my throat. It was a very sad day.

September

Horse & Pony magazine had contacted us the previous year and offered to run a 'Global Campaign' on our work, the work of the ILPH and that of the British Horse Society. During the year they featured various articles on the three charities to raise money for their work. They specifically featured our work in Mexico and their readers had generously raised funds and sent donations to the magazine. To our delight they had raised a magnificent amount, and they presented Dawn with a cheque for £14,643 at Burleigh Horse Trials.

June and I departed on a much-needed holiday to the Scilly Isles. This was our second visit. On our first visit when we were eighteen years old, we had sailed across such rough seas on the *Scillonian* that I had been badly seasick and it took me all week to recover! This time we travelled by helicopter, and we spent relaxing days walking and enjoying the beautiful gardens. The only disappointment of the week was the practice in our hotel of seating newcomers at the back of the dining room and moving them forward each night as earlier guests left. We both hated having to find a different table and waiter each night, and only managed to get to the second row from the window on the last night. We never really felt settled, and found it a strange practice.

29th September was a great day, when we officially opened our Leeds EST Centre! Dame Thora Hird honoured us by performing the official ceremony, in the company of Councillor Denise Atkinson. Dame Thora gave a most delightful talk and a group of children with special needs performed a 'pantomime' of Cinderella, with a small girl named Lucy playing the title role. The most poignant moment was when the Prince, played by a little boy called Akleem, found Cinderella's slipper – a little shoe to fit a donkey, and he found the donkey who had lost it! It moved us all to tears! It was a lovely day for us all, particularly Debbie, and I was pleased to see my cousin, Derrick, and his wife, Betsy, playing a major part in the day. Derrick organised seating and generally looked after the guests, and Betsy was in charge of the catering, having made dozens of sandwiches and cakes! With his strong northern accent, Derrick said to me later, 'Ee, Bet – I think Debbie's going to be all right with you,' which certainly made me very happy. Dame Thora had been

The opening of the Leeds EST Centre.

such an asset to the day and, despite her increasing frailty, she happily agreed to be whisked off into Leeds later that day to give a wonderfully supportive talk about EST on Radio Leeds.

Four selected donkeys from the Leeds Centre were added to the Adoption Scheme: Rosie, Kelly, William D and Simon (pictures on p119). We now had twelve donkeys in the scheme, which kept the Adoption Department very busy.

We received some terrible news concerning the transportation of donkeys from Romania to Italy. Donkeys were being transported hundreds of miles in appalling conditions, but nothing had prepared Lionel Ford, our Welfare Officer, for the sight that met his eyes when, in co-operation with a European Charity named Animals Angels, he found and was able to follow two overloaded vehicles over a four-day journey from Romania through Hungary to Italy. One hundred and twenty donkeys were crowded into one lorry, with another 120 in a second. Three heavily pregnant mares foaled during the journey, and all three foals were trampled to death because the donkeys were packed in so tightly. One donkey was trapped under a partition for most of the journey and must have suffered indescribably. Paul immediately visited the areas concerned to see if there was anything we could do to stop this dreadful practice.

October

On one of my regular 'walkabouts' I visited the Isolation Unit with Michael Crane and a veterinary student who was 'seeing practice' at the Sanctuary. The manager of the unit, Glen Gardiner, introduced us to two new donkeys, Naomi and Jack. I must say Jack was well named. He spent the time I was there pacing up and down the fence, on the other side of which were two mares in season! There was no doubt that, once settled in, he was another donkey who would have to pay a visit to the veterinary department. Before I left the Isolation Unit I was introduced to the veterinary student, whose name was Bryony, and I was amazed to learn that she was the daughter of the wonderful lady

Tiny Titch

who took Tiny Titch and So Shy into her care all those years ago! During her stay, Bryony was delighted to be able to meet up with Tiny Titch again at Town Barton Farm and I'm sure that the feeling was mutual!

Radar's owners ran a pub and she had been fed on leftover food from the meals served to their customers. As a result she became extremely overweight and this, together with the fact that her feet were not good, meant she spent a lot of time lying down. There was very little grass in her paddock and, to make matters worse, there was ragwort everywhere. Radar's owners felt they could no longer look after her, and they sent her into our care. Due to her weight problem and the fact that she may possibly already have been poisoned by ragwort, her future prospects seemed bleak from a veterinary point of view. In fact she died only three years later. Ragwort is a real killer, and the Sanctuary spearheaded a campaign along with the National Equine Welfare Council (NEWC) and other equine charities to point out its dangers to the general public. We also co-operate with many local councils and the Ministry of Agriculture to keep this poisonous weed under control.

I wrote another little poem for Memorial Day, prompted by my visit a few evenings earlier to see the geriatric donkeys in New Barn. As I sat beside one of the old ladies, stroking her lovely soft muzzle, I felt inspired! I felt unable to recite the poem on the day, as I always seem to end up crying, but Richard Barnes readily agreed to do the honours!

It's quiet at night in the donkeys' barn
The silence disturbed by a rustle
As an elderly donkey slowly lies down
Protected from life's daily bustle.
Her eyes may be dim as she lays on the straw
Outstretched, her flanks hardly moving
Thoughts of before filled with fear and with pain
Of a past life, which is slowly improving.
Does she sleep, as we do, through the hours of the night?
Is she able to escape from her past?
Or is she forever doomed to remember
Awake, till the dawn comes at last?
Should we, as her carers, feel guilt and remorse
That our species can be inhumane?
That cruelty comes in a daily dose

Inflicted to cause greatest pain.
This seems the moment, as we're gathered here
To remember their suffering today
And just take a moment to think of them all
And for that poor old donkey to pray.

November

I paid a very sad visit to Honiton hospital, to see Charles Judge. Charles had been the Sanctuary's first Welfare Officer and had been of tremendous help to me over the years in my quest to help as many donkeys in the UK as possible. Unfortunately Charles was terminally ill, but he was mentally alert and delighted to see me. We discussed the old days together, and he spoke proudly of the fact that his name would be carried on at the Sanctuary through his son, David, who was also a Welfare Officer.

One of the very well known Donkey Breed Society champions, Barnabas of Grove Hill, had been with us for many years. He was one of only three donkeys allowed to remain as a stallion at the Sanctuary, as a pronounced heart murmur detected on his arrival meant an operation was too dangerous for him. His owner, Dorothy Morris, had been a friend of mine since my days as a member of the Donkey Breed Society. I was so shocked to hear from my vets that Barnabas had suffered a stroke, and his condition was rapidly deteriorating. I telephoned Dorothy straight away, and she was able to be with him in his final few hours. It never ceases to amaze me how, even after many years, donkeys recognise their former owners and, although Barnabas had refused to take any special treats from the staff, Dorothy offered him a rich tea biscuit and he accepted it – he knew she was there! Barnabas, who was well over thirty-six when he died, had not only had a good life – he'd also had a good death.

December

The Irish Sanctuary received a lovely Christmas gift this year. A Christmas gift from one of our supporters to his wife was a donation to build a hospital at the Sanctuary! We were so very grateful, as this would be of such benefit to the donkeys, and plans were put in hand to get the project started early next year.

I usually go away over Christmas and New Year, but this year was different. There was widespread concern around the world that computer systems would not be able to cope with the change of date to the new millennium, so Paul and I agreed we should stay on duty over the holiday period. Although I knew that Paul would be able to cope well with any problems, the consequences of losing the computerised records of our donkeys and those of our loyal supporters would be disastrous, and I felt that I should be there to give Paul any assistance he needed.

During the evening of Christmas Day I walked across the yards towards New Barn. All was peaceful – just the gentle rhythmic noise of ninety donkeys chewing came from inside. The interior was illuminated by the infra-red lights, warming the donkeys' backs and radiating a soft red glow. I stood quietly just inside the door watching the donkeys with their heads in the feeders, so calm and peaceful after the ordeals many of them had suffered earlier in their lives. One by one they raised their heads and looked at me, with little noises of recognition. Then all but two of them put their heads down again and continued munching. The two donkeys came up to me and I didn't need to look at their collars to know their names. Merlin and Susie were obviously still missing their loving owners. They nuzzled against me and we shared a wonderful moment on that special evening.

2 0 0 0
FLOODS AND FOALS

January

I mentioned earlier the discussions that had taken place with regard to incorporating the IDPT into the Donkey Sanctuary. With the permission of the Charity Commission, at the Trustees meeting held on 18th January, a formal resolution was passed that, at midnight of 30th September 2000, IDPT would pass over all its funds to the Donkey Sanctuary. The Donkey Sanctuary would then take control of all the overseas work in addition to its work in the UK. The Trustees of the IDPT – my sister Pat, Professor Jimmy Duncan, Bill Jordan, Bill Tetlow and Rosalind de Wesselow – passed a similar resolution in their meeting the following day. Following the incorporation it was decided that the title of 'Administrator' should be changed: I became Chief Executive and Paul and Mal became Deputy Chief Executives of the Donkey Sanctuary.

While we were sad that the IDPT would no longer be functioning in its own right, everyone agreed that the administration work and costs would be greatly reduced, and this in turn would enable more funds to be put towards our overseas work. With over 56 million donkeys in the world this was recognised to be of vital importance. Although the IDPT would no longer be an active charity, the Charity Commission suggested that it should remain on their register so that any monies which had been bequeathed to that charity from a Will could still be claimed. Any funds received in this way would immediately be passed over to the Donkey Sanctuary, and these would be used specifically for overseas work to comply with the restricted funding regulations.

At the Donkey Sanctuary Trustees' meeting I suggested that a very useful addition to the board would be David Cook, who, you may remember, I had got to know well while cruising on the *Arcadia*. David was at the time the Group Finance Director for Millennium and Copthorne Hotels plc. I felt his expertise would be invaluable in coping with the constantly changing rules and regulations in accounting practices, in addition to his obvious interest in the welfare of donkeys. The Trustees agreed, and it was decided that David should join the board immediately following the incorporation of the IDPT into the Donkey Sanctuary in October.

February

I attended a meeting of the Welfare Fund for Companion Animals in the House of Lords, and was able to report that, following an appeal in our Newsletter, we had been able to raise over £2,000 in specific funds for the Companion Animal Welfare Council. The council had sent out calls for evidence to local authorities, the police, animal welfare organisations and individuals with particular expertise relating to the first two work studies to be progressed. Committees were set up to co-ordinate each work study: Lou Leather of the Pet Advisory Committee was elected as chairman for the study on the Identification and Registration of Companion Animals, and the study on Standards and Controls for Companion Animal Rescue Establishments was to be jointly chaired by Professor Neil Gorman and Baroness Wharton.

A low-key official opening ceremony for the Trow Farm office block took place this month. I cut a ribbon and gave a brief talk, after which all who attended adjourned to the new Welfare/Admissions Department for soft drinks and sandwiches. The office in Honiton was closed, and Paul, Richard and staff were able to move into their new offices. Other departments which moved to Trow Farm were the Welfare Department, the 'Post Out' Department, and Sue Hudson with her EST Adoption team. One of the barns at Trow Farm was converted to a 'Stores', under the capable supervision of Paul Rockey, and a small electric van was purchased for transporting supplies between the two offices.

At the end of the month the veterinary department held its first Continuing Professional Development (CPD) meeting in conjunction with the British Equine Veterinary Association (BEVA) and the University of Bristol at their Department of Clinical Veterinary Science at Langford. I had the honour of opening the meeting, and the speakers included Andrew Trawford, Michael Crane, Stuart Reid, Jane French (animal behaviourist) and Nora Matthews, a well-known expert in anaesthesia from the USA. There were around eighty attendees. I was pleased to see executives from other animal welfare charities were there, and they joined in the lively question and answer session at the end of the day. A copy of the *Professional Handbook of the Donkey* was given to each delegate at the end of the day, and I felt it was an excellent way of promoting awareness of the donkey's needs to vets in the field.

Mr Downton, a Weymouth beach donkey operator, and his family had been giving donkey rides on the beach for 120 years through three generations. Our Welfare Officer, Lionel Ford, said that Mr Downton was one of the very best beach operators in the UK; his standards were excellent and his donkeys were much loved and well cared for. However, the time had now come for Mr Downton to retire and he was concerned about the future of his precious donkeys. We already had Chuck, Raindrop and Candy in our care, as Mr Downton always retired his donkeys when they reached the age of eighteen years. He contacted us and of course we readily agreed to take his seventeen donkeys into the Sanctuary. It was an historic and emotional day for him when we arrived to collect his donkeys. All seventeen donkeys settled in well, and would no doubt enjoy their retirement with us.

March

My grand-daughter Dawn was progressing with her career within the charity. In 1998 she became a PR assistant and was promoted to PR officer in 1999. I admired her wonderful enthusiasm and she enjoyed drawing the attention of the media to our work by issuing press releases on events as they occurred at the Sanctuary.

I was pleased to hear from Dawn that the Channel 4 programme 'Pet Rescue' was coming to film at the Donkey Sanctuary. In all the crew spent three weeks at the Sanctuary, filming five different aspects of our work, each of which would be shown within the 'Pet Rescue' programmes during one week early in 2000. The areas filmed were:

1. The work of EST, featuring Ellen Tinkham School, which had been bringing children to the Slade Centre for many years. Also featured was the work of our Donkey Facilitated Therapy Unit.
2. Work in the donkey hospital, including an operation on a donkey, and our vet nurses making 'sandwiches' for the donkeys. We've found that donkeys are happy to take their medication if sandwiched between slices of bread or ginger nut biscuits!
3. Assessing donkeys' suitability to go out into a foster home and giving individual training in our Training Centre. Robbie and Noel were the donkeys filmed, and their arrival at their new home was featured.
4. The Show team, featuring Boomer, who was being trained in the disciplines necessary to be taken to shows and exhibitions.
5. Featuring Moppet, a donkey at Woods Farm. When Moppet came into our care her owners, Mr and Mrs Dann, moved house to be near her.

Part of Mal's executive duties is overseeing the Irish Sanctuary, which continued to take into its care donkeys that were the subject of cruelty and neglect. Together with Paddy Barrett, she was able to set up a welfare officer network in Ireland and was busy organising good foster homes for donkeys there. By now, 1,689 donkeys had been taken into care in Ireland and the Sanctuary was becoming full to capacity.

Mal, along with Jacqueline Gosden and Maggie Taylor, was also largely responsible for organising a club for children aged between 5 and 12 years. 'Donkidz' members receive a bumper information pack about donkeys, including pen, poster, badge, eraser, sticker and two Newsletters a year. Membership is £5 and, once joined, children are then members until they reach their 13th birthday. The aim of 'Donkidz' is to make children aware of donkey welfare, which we feel is important and will help to ensure that children grow into adulthood with the knowledge of donkeys' needs. Education of future generations is a vital part of our work.

April

My latest book, *The Story of Tiny Titch*, was published in April, and I was delighted with the result! Eve Bygrave had agreed to do the illustrations for the book and they were lovely. Eve has illustrated many of my children's books over the years, and I enjoyed her visit to the Sanctuary, when photographs were taken so that she could paint the pictures of Tiny Titch and the Hayloft Restaurant as accurately as possible. Children everywhere seem to love stories of naughty donkeys and each story has an element of truth in it, although I must admit, with my imagination, I sometimes get carried away!

The next CEBEC meeting was held at a gentleman's club in London, and John Stoker, the Chief Charity Commissioner, was invited to join us for lunch. Arriving at the club, I was surprised when my knock was answered by a gentleman who said, 'I'm sorry, Madam. We don't admit ladies,' and promptly closed the door again. I was standing there wondering what to do next, when Peter Davies arrived. He said, 'I'm so sorry, Betty. There's been a misunderstanding. Do come in.' No-one had considered the fact that it was a gentlemen's club – and they were not happy about bending the rules for me! I understand that the Queen Mother had the same trouble when she'd visited; Her Majesty was relegated to the basement for dinner – and the same happened to the CEBEC members, because of me! I don't know to this day whether I should have felt honoured to be allowed in or annoyed that there were still clubs in existence that excluded women! I've heard since, however, that the rules of the club have been relaxed somewhat, in that ladies are now allowed in – but on one floor only!

I never get over the miracle of birth – especially where donkeys are

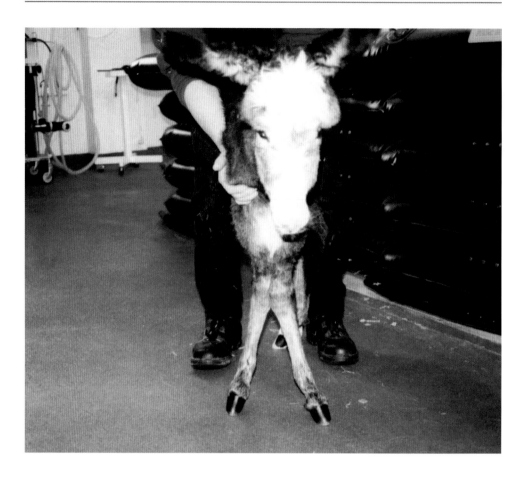

Peanuts – born with twisted legs.

concerned. We knew we could face problems with some 'in foal' mares we had rescued jointly with the RSPCA; the mares had been badly treated and this could have a bad effect on their foaling. Two foals had already been born over the Easter period. We were keeping an eye on the remainder of the group, looking for the tell-tale signs of imminent birth. The next donkey found to be in foal was Nina at Woods Farm and we decided that she should stay at the farm until the foal was born rather than risking stress by moving her nearer to the hospital. Unfortunately, when the foal was born, both her front legs were twisted, so mother and baby had to be brought back to Slade House Farm. The foal's physical problem was exacerbated by the fact that her mother did not accept her, which caused us even more concern. Almost twenty-five years ago I'd experienced an identical problem with a new-born foal when my husband and I were running the Salston Hotel at Ottery St Mary. I had called that little foal 'Peanuts', so we immediately gave this new foal the same name. Dedicated nursing ensured Peanuts' survival; bottle feeds were given every two hours night and day, while Nina stood watching, apparently quite happy to let us do the work. The vets were wonderful; Alex and Vicky carefully made splints for Peanuts' front legs, changing them daily until it was clear that the treatment was working. When the splints were finally removed after ten days, Peanuts was able to stand unaided and a few days later she enjoyed her first outing in one of the hospital paddocks.

I wish we'd had the same success with the next birth. We were very aware that, due to the donkeys' poor condition on arrival, the mares could be in trouble and the foals could have problems, and for poor Freda this was the case. Normally the birth takes place very quickly once labour starts, but Freda was struggling from the outset and, despite veterinary help, the foal was born dead – a devastating result for both Freda and us.

Within a short time, a little colt foal was born to Emma, with no complications at birth, but with physical problems! This time the foal couldn't stand. With both his back legs twisted and weak, he lay in a corner, unable to stand and feed. Happily his mother loved him straight away, and, with staff holding him to the 'milk bar', he drank well and strongly. Once more Alex and Vicky made special splints, and I'm afraid that, after watching him trying to stand, I named him 'Bandy'! He had a further problem in that his bones were under-developed but, with the help of the splints and a tiny corrective shoe, Bandy has come on, quite literally, in leaps and bounds.

Eventually there was one more mare of the group left to foal. Zebina grew fatter and fatter, and we spent many hours watching her in case there were problems. The vets were concerned, but we decided to wait and let nature take its course.

May

I was pleased to announce during Donkey Week that we had been invited to put on a display at the Devon County Show in May next year. At this early stage discussions were being held between key members of staff as to what form the demonstration should take, and I felt this would be an ideal opportunity to bring to the UK some of the vets working on our overseas projects. They could take part in the display, hopefully in their national costumes and, whilst here, could also undertake additional training in donkey welfare. This would be a massive undertaking, and I knew it would take a lot of planning.

A phone call from Lord Soulsby left me devastated, as he told me that Baroness Wharton was terminally ill. I couldn't believe that such a vibrant, bubbly person had been struck down with an appalling illness for which there was no cure. Ziki (as I knew her) was an endless campaigner for animal welfare rights in the House of Lords and was, in fact, one of the few hereditary peers to be elected to remain in the House of Lords as a result of the government's 'shake-up'. As an original member of the steering group, she'd played a major role in the setting up of CAWC. Sadly she died at the end of May, and I knew that she would be missed by everyone who knew her. I also realised that losing Ziki would affect the completion of the study already in progress.

June

Paul and I received an invitation from the Spanish Ambassador to attend a cocktail party to say farewell to Rafael Cavestany, whose posting in the UK was about to finish. I wasn't really looking forward to it, as I'm not very good at sipping drinks and making small talk, but I felt that we had to keep the good relationship going in the hope that eventually the Ambassador would be able to do something about the terrible Fiesta in Villanueva de la Vera. We arrived to find the grounds of the Embassy already full of foreign diplomats and VIPs, and both Paul and I felt rather out of place. Everyone seemed to know each other and the groups were chattering in what I would term as 'little huddles'. We stood alone sipping our drinks and were pleased when a very pleasant lady broke away from a group and came to talk to us. She seemed very interested in our work and, after a few moments, the Ambassador joined us and introduced the lady as his wife, the Marquesa de Tamaron. The subject of the fiesta was introduced, and the Ambassador promised to give us all the support he could. On the way to the party I'd received news from the Sanctuary that Zebina had just produced a filly foal and, on the spur of the moment, I suggested that she should be named after the Marquesa. As the Ambassador led his wife to greet other guests, she turned to me and said emotionally, 'I would be really honoured if you would call the little foal Tamaron.'

When Paul and I arrived back at the Sanctuary we went straight to Zebina's stable. Tamaron was a beautiful jet black foal and, more importantly, she appeared to have no problems. It seemed that the extra time and care Zebina had received since coming into the Sanctuary had enabled her to make up for her earlier lack of nourishment. To see their happiness, and knowing they could stay together safely for life brought tears to my eyes.

July

Things have changed in the farming world since I founded the Sanctuary. I'm sure everyone knows about conventional hay bales, but now we have 'big round bales' and even D1000 bales! To give you an idea of sizes: there are 8-10 conventional bales in a big round bale, and 12 in a D1000 bale! Donkeys don't like the type of hay that horses love. They prefer the grass to have seeded and become rather coarse, preferably with a few juicy thistles in! As a result we make our hay later than all our neighbouring farmers, and the weather plays an all-important role. On Slade House Farm we make around 6-7,000 conventional bales, which are useful as we have so many individual donkey boxes and intensive care stables. We employ contractors to make the big bales, as we don't have the necessary machinery. We often make haylage as well, which is a mix between hay and silage. The advantage of haylage is that it is dried for a shorter period than hay, and creates less dust for the donkeys with breathing difficulties. Of course, many of our geriatric donkeys have few or no teeth; their feed has to be soft bran mashes or a special high fibre feed. It's surprising how the old donkeys tuck in, though, with much circling around the bucket to ensure no other 'oldie' steals any!

June and I enjoy our hobbies, among which is collecting antiques. Recently I've found that when I start collecting certain pieces the price is very reasonable, but as time goes on the price goes up. We always enjoy going to antique fairs, our favourite venue being at Shepton Mallet in Somerset. The Donkey Sanctuary receives all sorts of jewellery and antiques, often left to the charity in a will or sent to us as a donation, and it has become routine that I take these to antique fairs to sell them at the best possible price on behalf of the charity. I'm amazed at how kind the dealers can be; their initial reaction is often that they're not interested in what I have to offer but, upon hearing that it's for the Donkey Sanctuary, they change their minds and make a generous offer! I've made lots of friends within the antiques trade – and gained more supporters in the process!

I'm also keen on caring for the birds in my large aviary, many of which are rescued. I have a large variety of different species, some of which are quite rare, and it's fascinating to watch them build nests and lay their eggs. Unfortunately some of the larger birds think they have the right to help themselves to the precious eggs, so I decided to treat myself to an incubator in which the eggs can hatch and I can have the

Bourke's parrakeet.

pleasure of nurturing the tiny chicks until I can re-introduce them safely into the aviary.

I was very sad to lose three key members of staff during the year. John Rabjohns, one of the managers of Slade House Farm, retired in May. John had been such a great help to me and the donkeys for many years, and I was sad to see him go. Julie and Charles Courtney had decided to take early retirement, and they left the Sanctuary at the end of July. Julie had been an essential part of my work since the very early days, becoming Principal of the Slade Centre when Pat retired. Charles had managed Brookfield Farm before becoming Chief Welfare Officer. I knew we would miss them all.

When our family get-togethers occur during the summer I always try to arrange some sort of entertainment, and this year it was a 'mission nearly impossible'! I gave each team an instruction sheet, a camera with ten exposures and an envelope containing some money, and off they went. They had to take photographs as listed below:

1. Ottery St Mary Church clock
2. Escot House
3. A plane on the ground at Exeter Airport
4. A boat on the shingle at Beer
5. Sidmouth sea front
6. Coombe House Hotel
7. Salcombe Regis Church
8. A donkey at the Sanctuary
9. The team eating ice creams on a bank
10. The team on the steps at Weston beach

The money was needed for items which they had to bring back:

1. A ticket for fuel for £9.99 (or any amount ending in 99 pence

(with one point deducted for each 1p wrong)
2.   The same number of ice cream wrappers as there were people in the team
3.   Any 'Tesco' brand item
4.   A 'loyalty card' from Escot House
5.   Half a toilet roll
6.   A crab shell
7.   A seagull's feather
8.   A beer mat
9.   A conker

While the teams were on their mission I stayed at home preparing a meal for us all and, once again, we had a lovely day.

Following a CEBEC meeting in Newcastle, June and I travelled north

My children: (from left to right) *Lise, Paul, Clive and Sarah.*

for three days in the Mennock river searching for gold again. The sight of each other in our oilskins often made us laugh. On one occasion June was knocked over by the rushing water. Her oilskins immediately filled with water and she floated downstream like 'Mr Blobby in green'! We were hysterical with laughter and could hardly manage to drag ourselves out of the water. Our panning was more successful on this visit, and by the time we left, we had collected sufficient gold to put with our earlier findings and were able to have a pendant made for me and a ring for June. I treasure the result of our labours and it brings back many happy memories.

On our way back from Scotland we called at Newton Farm where Ray and Julie were holding their Open Day. The farm was, as usual, immaculate, and they had a lovely day in store for their visitors. It was good to see all our friends, including David and Jill Cook, as usual running a stall to raise funds for the Sanctuary. Janet and Peter Thorne were running another stall, and I was pleased to be able to thank them personally for the amazing amount of money they have raised over the years – they are a truly remarkable couple, and I will never be able to thank them enough for their help. As I left I congratulated Ray and Julie on their successful day. I was most upset then to learn that Ray's health had been causing them concern and his doctor feared he had developed Parkinson's disease. I crossed my fingers that this wasn't the case, but we'd just have to wait and see.

August

The EST Festival was held at the Leeds Centre this year, and was a tremendous success. The only problem was that access to the Centre is along a single track lane, and around 10,000 visitors turned up, resulting in chaos in the lane when departing visitors found the lane was blocked by others trying to get to the Centre. We had warned the police that there might be heavy traffic in the lanes that day, but I don't think they took us seriously and only one policeman turned up. Luckily we were able to contact the farmer who owned the adjoining land and he kindly allowed us to direct the outgoing traffic through his fields, which eased the problem immediately.

All the EST Trustees attended the Festival and we arranged to hold our Trustees' meeting at the Centre the following day. They were all thrilled with the success of the Festival and of the Centre itself, which was fully booked by special needs' schools in the area. I didn't want them to rest on our laurels though – I already had a fourth Centre in mind! There was much discussion on where this should be situated, and the suggestions were whittled down to four – Manchester, Cardiff, Plymouth or Glasgow. It was agreed that research would be undertaken on each area, after which a decision would be made. Having a fourth Centre in mind meant, of course, that some more serious fundraising had to be done and I returned to Devon with this uppermost in my mind.

My youngest daughter, Sarah, was living happily with her partner, Paul, in Greenwich, and I spent a lovely weekend with them in late August. Both had jobs in the City where Sarah was working with a family-run printing company and Paul was involved in producing computer games. Although they are both fond of cooking – Sarah having qualified as a chef at the Pru Leith College – I managed to treat them to a meal out. We went to a Chinese restaurant and I think we tried every dish on the menu! It was lovely to see them so happy together.

September
I made my annual visit to Denmark to see Lise and her family in September. My grandson, Mark, wasn't at home as he was doing a course in business studies at the University of Plymouth. My grand-daughter, Kate, had not been too well, but we were able to do some shopping in Aarhus and Randers, and I thoroughly enjoyed my few days with them.

October
On 1st October the IDPT formally handed its work over to the Donkey Sanctuary and at their meeting shortly afterwards the Trustees were pleased to welcome David Cook onto the board.

To thank the Trustees of IDPT for their many years of voluntary work for the charity, I asked Lord Soulsby if he would be kind enough to arrange for them all to have lunch in the House of Lords, followed by a tour. He was happy to oblige, and they all enjoyed a wonderful day, which concluded with a trip on the London Eye.

I had a very moving experience a few years ago when I saw a little girl brought into the Slade Centre on a mobile bed so that she could see the donkeys. Recalling this one day I was inspired to write a poem for Memorial Day which, even now, brings tears to my eyes:

I just can't move my arms and legs
I really don't know why
My Mum keeps saying 'please stand up'
And I do my best to try.
The days seem long, and I get tired
Lying on a bed all day
If only something nice could happen
I close my eyes and pray.
For seven long years I've been like this
Though my mind is really clear
I can't understand why my legs won't work
And the adults say 'Never mind, dear'.
But something happened yesterday
That has brought some hope to me
They lifted me into the family car
And they drove to a place near the sea.
They wheeled my bed through a great big door
And they gave me a terrible fright
Because in came an animal, oh so big
Who stood by me, and blocked out the light.
He put down his head and touched my hand
His breath was all warm and wet
I could feel his soft hair brushing my arm
It was a feeling I'd come to forget.
I longed to reach out and touch the long ears
And I longed to get out of my bed
It was joy that I felt, as they lifted me up
And then put a hard hat on my head.
And then, oh the thrill, I was up on his back
Looking down on my Mum and my Dad
But why was Mum crying, and holding my hand
When I was feeling so glad?
The tingle I'd felt in my arm had come back –
I could feel a strange buzz in my feet
And I tried and I tried to sit up straight
On my wonderful donkey so sweet.
But then it was over and back on the ground
They held me as close as they could
For I longed and I prayed I could touch his soft nose
And my hands knew that they really should.

He nuzzled my hand, and my fingers uncurled
And my arm moved the very first time
And my tears wet his face as I knew that at last
With his help, God had given a sign.

Throughout my life I've felt that someone was guiding me. Although I'm not particularly religious, it seems incredible to me that all my dreams and wishes miraculously come true.

The autumn brought about the dramatic rescue of Swifty. Shelagh Steel, one of our Regional Welfare Officers, received a call from Robin Porter, a Welfare Officer from the ILPH, with regard to the terrible plight of a donkey caught in floodwater. The initial call for help had come via the RSPCA and the 'Animal Hospital' television programme, and it appeared that 'donkey experts' were urgently required. Swifty's owner lived in Hillingdon, Middlesex, and Swifty had lived in an adjoining field. Many years before he had wandered off, crossing a small river when it was almost dry, to arrive on a tiny island which he decided would be his future home! His owner had to cross a rickety bridge to feed him, and even she became a target for an angry Swifty, who hated anyone to come onto his island! During the appallingly bad weather in November the island was rapidly disappearing under floodwater. Paul and Ben Hart, our donkey behaviourist, were called to the rescue!

Apparently the only ways off the island at the time were over a wooden slatted bridge, which would not take the donkey's weight, or over a narrow concrete bridge – and Swifty would cross neither! Attempts by the RSPCA, the ILPH and even the local fire brigade had failed. On arrival, whilst Ben tried to win Swifty's confidence, Paul walked around the island and, to his joy, he found a spot where there was only a narrow stretch of water and an easily breached fence that led to the local sailing club. However, by the time darkness approached Ben had managed to get Swifty to move only 50 yards, and they were nowhere near the fence.

The water had risen substantially the following morning. The concrete bridge was entirely under water and the strip of water adjacent to the sailing club was twice the width and depth. The sailing club opened up its dinghy park and allowed Paul to take down part of the fence. He explained to onlookers that the members of the club would be relieved if the donkey could be moved. For many years owners of any dinghies or boats that went aground on the island had to face a charging donkey who both bit and kicked those unfortunate enough to be on his property. Ben's efforts were at last bearing fruit, and he and Swifty seemed to be coming to some arrangement after the quiet, calm negotiations. The film crew gave Paul and Ben until 1pm to walk Swifty off, otherwise it was going to be a case for a helicopter rescue, and Swifty would certainly find that stressful. But Ben managed the impossible and at 12.58 they waded together through the rising water and Swifty was saved. The rescue was featured in the 'Animal Hospital' programme later that month.

November

I regularly visit my ex-husband's stepfather, Svend, who has lived in Exeter for most of his life. Sadly both his first and second wives had died from cancer, and he now lived on his own. Following a nasty fall, Svend became increasingly frail and, as he wanted to remain in his own home, I was able to arrange 24-hour care for him, with qualified 'carers' always on hand. Now 96 years old, his brain is as acute as ever, and it's a pleasure to chat with him on a wide range of subjects. His memory is quite amazing (see picture on page 199).

Although I know all donkeys are lovely, some do cause us headaches! As you can imagine, with so many donkeys there is a large amount of dung and dirty water to dispose of, and the drains run under the yards, with special drain covers over the inspection chambers. Each drain cover has a small hook – and this was the cause of the trouble! Mal, who lived in Buffalo Barn at the time, developed a favourite trick. He would wrap his tongue around the hook, then grab it with his teeth and pull! Having removed the cover, his friends would join him to gaze in wonderment down the deep hole! As a result, our maintenance team had to saw off all the hooks and drill holes through which a rod could be inserted to lift the lid. Mal didn't bother to work this one out – he turned his attention to trying to remove the padlock from the gates, while at the same time trying to keep out of the way of Peter – another resident donkey in Buffalo Barn. Peter's favourite trick was to manoeuvre himself between the shafts of the wheelbarrow (often full of dung!) and push it around the yard. He often collided with other unsuspecting donkeys in his effort to tip it up in the most inaccessible place!

We always do as much as we can to make new donkeys feel at home when they first arrive in our Isolation Unit. One day I saw a donkey in

Enjoying the winter sunshine.

'Jake the Peg', with one boot missing. However, I learned that Jake had loved his owners dearly, and shortly after his arrival they came to visit, bringing one of their boots as a keepsake! Jake carried it everywhere with him! Apparently when Jake first came into the sanctuary his former owners used to phone him; a member of staff would hold a mobile phone to Jake's ear while he stood quietly and listened to the nice things they had to say!

We lost another precious member of our staff in November. Denis Shepherd had been a loyal member of the Adoption Department for several years, and had worked previously in other departments. His death was sudden. I felt so sorry for his daughter, Fiona, as her father had taken the greatest care of her since the death of his wife when Fiona was very young and they were extremely close. Fiona was a long-serving member of our staff and has efficiently manned the switchboard since 1983. Happily she had married a few years' ago and now had a young daughter, Bronte, so I was re-assured that Fiona would have lots of loving support. She misses her father desperately, though, and I was happy to agree that a plaque should be erected in the rose garden, through which Fiona passes each morning to come into the office.

December

This year we designed a Christmas card with a difference! These were mailed out to our supporters with the Autumn Newsletter in November. In this card was a picture of a carrot, which could be pushed out and sent back with a donation for EST. The returned carrots were then used to decorate the Christmas tree standing in each of the Centres. Not only did they make interesting and unusual decorations, the funds raised far exceeded our expectations.

'Animal Hospital' asked if they could film at the Sanctuary just before Christmas, and we were pleased to co-operate. Arrangements were made to film a Nativity Play presented by Sidmouth Infants School in our Harvey Barn at Hurfords. Although Rolf Harris wasn't able to come, co-presenters Rhodri Williams and Edwina Silver were there to present the programme. I immediately noticed the wonderful rapport Rhodri had with the children, immediately putting them at ease. It set me wondering whether he might be prepared to become a Patron of EST. Spike Milligan, who had been a Patron of the Slade Centre, had recently died and I felt it would be good for EST to have the name of a celebrity attached to it. I decided to ask Rhodri later whether he would take on this role.

2 0 0 1
FOOT AND MOUTH DISEASE
AND MORE BROKEN BONES!

January

June and I arrived back from our Christmas cruise on the *Aurora* to bitterly cold weather in Sidmouth. I soon warmed up, however, as I went into the office and saw the piles of paperwork and reports waiting for me. Before starting I took the opportunity to walk around the yard amongst my lovely donkeys. I'm always quite worried that, on my return, some of my old friends will have gone, as of course many of them were now becoming elderly. I always like to be with them when the end comes, to give them a hug and a ginger biscuit and say goodbye to them properly. However, this time I was fortunate, and I was able to return to my office happy that all was well.

The preparations for the display at Devon County Show in May were well underway, and I was delighted to learn that Dame Thora Hird was willing to take part in our display. We had decided to concentrate on our rapidly growing overseas work, and Margaret Farrow, secretary in the Overseas Department, was by now busy organising flights and accommodation for all those coming in from other countries. Jacqueline Gosden had built up a very good rapport with the show officials, and they had kindly offered us an excellent position, free of charge, within the showground to site our exhibition stand and static display. We were delighted to be offered prime time in the main arena for our principal display, which was to be entitled 'Working for Donkeys around the World'. Thora Hird and I were to lead the procession, arriving in the arena in a donkey cart. We were to be followed by presentations from all our overseas clinics, a parade of beach donkeys, a display by the children with special needs who attend the Sidmouth EST Centre, and displays by our Donkey Facilitated Therapy Unit, driving teams, representatives from The Donkey Breed Society, some of our well-known donkeys with interesting stories, and our beautiful 15-hand Poitou donkeys! On each of the three days of the show there would be smaller donkey displays in our own dedicated area.

February

I reported our plans to the Trustees at their meeting. Following the meeting I took them all to Paccombe Farm, where the donkeys' wintering yards had been covered. The winter months must seem a terribly long time to the donkeys as, apart from their warm, airy barns, they only have access to 'run-out' yards, and it is quite difficult to persuade them to take much-needed exercise in inclement weather. Paul felt this would be much more achievable if the yards were roofed, and it would also help us enormously to comply with the regulations on 'dirty water' set by the Environment Agency. With such large numbers of animals congregated in one area it was extremely difficult to avoid effluent seeping into streams or rivers where it could damage the natural environment, but rainwater running from the roofs would not be contaminated. The Trustees agreed that it was encouraging to see how contented the donkeys were with their new shelter.

March

I was having more problems with my stomach, and was told it could be induced by stress (and there is certainly plenty of that in my job!). I decided to take a break to a country with excellent medical facilities and food I could eat.

I booked a holiday to Disney World, Orlando – a new park had been opened there called 'Animal Kingdom' with donkeys in one of the areas. I knew I would be able to visit them whilst on holiday and would not be deprived of seeing donkeys! June was working in Mexico and her journey involved changing planes in Miami. This meant she could join me for the second week!

I left for Heathrow, Terminal 4, on the 29th March. I had booked a seat in 'Business Class' with Virgin Atlantic, as I often have a great deal of pain flying and need to get as flat as possible to alleviate this. We boarded on time and I stowed my hand luggage on the storage rack above my seat. I had a window seat.

I was quite excited as the plane revved up its engine and started off down the runway. To my horror a flash of fire ran along the cabin lockers and a curtain two rows behind me burst into flames! Oxygen masks suddenly descended followed by a shower of water! Despite the increasing acceleration those sitting by the curtain had no choice but to stand up; shouts of 'FIRE!' came from us all and within seconds one of the stewards rushed forward with a fire extinguisher and put the flames out. Suddenly we were all pushed forward in our seat belts as the brakes were applied. We had been right on the point of take off and swerved off the runway with the reverse engines on full thrust. The smell in the cabin was terrible and we were still being watered from above! As we came to a standstill, I could see fire engines on both sides of the plane, and as we stopped one drove right up to the window. What a relief to be stationary. I thought they would open the doors straight away – we were all quite keen to get out! – but we had to wait at least ten long minutes; apparently they were afraid the draught could re-ignite the fire. A cheery fireman's eyes met mine through the window and I moved back so that he could see into the cabin. When the doors opened at last, the cabin filled with about fifteen firemen – I nearly had one on my lap as he quickly threw all the hand baggage onto the floor! What an experience!

We were off-loaded onto a fleet of buses (there must have been about 300 passengers on the plane) and then taken back to the terminal where we waited – minus hand luggage – for almost seven hours! We eventually set off to re-board the plane in the early evening – our hand baggage already placed in the racks over our seats although mine was rather wet!

Bless Virgin Atlantic! We were offered a free First Class return flight to any destination of our choice to be used within the next twelve months! This paid for my trip to visit my son Clive and his wife Grainne in September!

I really enjoyed the holiday to Disney World's Animal Kingdom. It was wonderful to spend some time with my donkey friends, although I was concerned that they were terribly bored as they were kept in a small (but spotlessly clean) area. The donkeys were also rather overweight. As I was unable to meet their carer, I have since written to the Park and made some suggestions. I also sent a copy of our *Professional Handbook of the Donkey*, for which I have received a very satisfactory reply. I believe the donkeys now have toys in their area and they are being taken for walks early morning and during the evening!

Everything was going so well at the Sanctuary – I had wonderful staff, loyal supporters and, for the first time, I felt we were beginning to win the battle to ensure the well-being of every donkey in the UK. Then disaster struck – foot and mouth disease. Unfortunately the beautiful county of Devon became the centre of an outbreak of this dreadful infectious disease. Sheep grazing a quarter of a mile from the Sanctuary were traced as original contacts and these were slaughtered by the middle of March, with a total of 1,400 animals from Salcombe Regis, Woodbury Salterton and Ottery St Mary. A final blow came when Town Barton Farm was declared to be in an infected area. All our farms used sheep as part of our parasite control programme and, despite moving hundreds from our land before the ban on livestock movement became effective, we were still left with over 140 sheep at Slade House Farm.

Whilst donkeys cannot catch foot and mouth disease, they can spread it as humans can, so every precaution was taken. They remained in their barns, with the exception of a few sick donkeys who would be in danger health-wise if deprived of grass. The Sanctuary was closed to visitors from the day of the livestock movement ban, and Paul and a team worked late into the night to protect us. Every entrance was protected by dips, which all staff had to use when walking between the office and the car park.

The Ministry of Agriculture asked if we could spare a vet, and Andrew Trawford returned early from Ethiopia to be seconded to the Ministry for an indefinite period. Having discussed the problems with both Ministry staff and veterinary officers it was decided that Donkey Week should be cancelled, as the visitors could unwittingly bring the virus to the Sanctuary or take it home. We felt we could not encourage visits to the area when so many animals were at risk and farmers were in such deep trouble.

This was the first time in eighteen years that Donkey Week would not take place, and it was a tremendous blow to us all. It also looked doubtful that Devon County Show would go ahead and, in view of the costs we were incurring in bringing vets to England from overseas, we decided to cancel our plans for the display there and then. Suddenly the months ahead looked empty and bleak – no Donkey Week to look forward to, no County Show and an eerie emptiness on the farm which would normally be bustling with visitors at this time of year.

April

During the next two months I only went to London once. Mal and John Carroll joined me for a vital meeting with our London lawyers to discuss our proposals to form a trading company. Formerly trading activities were contained within the charity and we had an agreement with the Inland Revenue to pay a notional amount of tax. However, the sales of our goods had expanded to such a degree that we had to set up a separate trading subsidiary. The planning and implementation of 'Donkey World Ltd' was an enormous undertaking and we had many months of hard work ahead.

Before I registered The Donkey Sanctuary as a Charity in 1973 I had collected 38 donkeys, many in desperate trouble. One of these was Amber, who was taken into our care on 10th June 1972. Amber had a foal we named Helen, and I was almost in tears when I realised who I was cuddling in the Isolation Unit on one of my visits – it was my Amber, with Helen right beside her! It was such a delight to see them looking so well. We'd let them go out to a really good foster home, where they lived very happily for fourteen years. However, the caring foster parents were worried that Amber was getting rather old, and they wanted them to come back to us so that veterinary help was on hand in case of problems. It was a lovely reunion – I'm sure they remembered me. Sadly, Amber died later in the year, but Helen has since joined the group of donkeys that visit residential homes – and she is a great favourite.

At the end of the month, June and Andrew made one of their regular visits to Lamu to carry out the regular donkey worming programme on the islands. While they were away I was thrilled to receive a letter from Professor Sandy Love of the University of Glasgow asking me if I would open BEVA's Annual Congress, which was due to be held in Glasgow in September next year. BEVA has over 2,000 members of the veterinary profession, and I knew that there would be more than 1,000 delegates at the congress. I was apprehensive as to how much interest there would be in the welfare of donkeys, as horses probably featured much more in their day-to-day work. However, having voiced my concerns to Sandy, he was adamant that all vets should be made aware of the donkey's needs, and I agreed to do it with great trepidation. This would have to be one of the best lectures I ever gave!

When Andrew phoned from Lamu I was longing to pass on my news, but it vanished from my mind within seconds when I heard what he had to tell me. June had suffered a really bad accident, and I almost cried as he described what had happened. June's foot had been giving her pain for several days, but she didn't think it was anything serious, and set off with Andrew to Pate Island, where they had treated the donkeys. Because of the tide, they then had a three-mile walk to the other side of the island, where the boat was waiting. As they walked June's foot became more and more painful. The guide accompanying them was riding a large, strong stallion donkey and he offered to let June ride. After going a short distance something must have stung the donkey, which immediately bucked, throwing June onto the sand. To Andrew's horror he could see immediately that, not only was June's ankle broken, it was also dislocated. Fortunately he was able to help immediately and, with great ingenuity he strapped a hoof rasp to each side of her ankle to keep it in place. June was carried the remainder of

Helen.

the journey and they returned immediately through elephant crossing to Lamu.

The hospital in Lamu didn't have sufficient equipment to treat June's injury, but an X-ray showed beyond doubt the extensive damage. Arrangements were made immediately to get June back home, but the journey must have been terrible. From Lamu she had to travel by boat to Manda Island for the flight to Wilson airport in Nairobi, followed by a car journey through the city to Nairobi international airport. The flight to England took a further nine hours and a driver was waiting to collect her from Heathrow for the journey home to Devon. How she managed it I don't know – it must have been agony.

Fortunately June is member of BUPA and she was immediately admitted to the Nuffield hospital in Exeter, but they couldn't operate straight away as they found an enormous fracture blister when they removed the splints. June eventually had her operation and, following a nine-day stay in hospital, she returned home to face weeks of recuperation.

May

The movement of animals was still restricted as a result of the foot and mouth disease crisis, when we received an urgent call from the RSPCA regarding a group of donkeys at a sanctuary in Leeds. The RSPCA felt that the animals, including horses and donkeys, were being neglected by the owner and they asked us to take the donkeys into our care. We contacted DEFRA, who agreed that we could collect the donkeys immediately. To minimise the risk of spreading foot and mouth disease we had to follow the same procedures as those for cattle and sheep hauliers, and the drivers were not allowed to get out of the lorries – not even for a comfort stop! We sent four drivers in two lorries, and they collected the fourteen donkeys, returning to Devon without allowing the donkeys off at any time. I was in the Isolation Unit when they arrived back at 7am expecting to see donkeys in a terrible condition but, with the exception of one very elderly, frail donkey, they trotted off the lorry in what our vets would call 'a reasonable condition'.

They seemed quite happy after their long journey, and settled well into their new quarters. A careful feeding regime was undertaken by the Isolation staff and the vets checked them regularly to ensure there were no after-effects. I knew that the donkeys' elderly owner was distraught at losing her animals, so I rang to tell her that they had all arrived safely, promising that I would keep in touch with her.

By the middle of May the foot and mouth disease problems were beginning to ease and, after 91 days, we were able to re-open the main part of the Donkey Sanctuary on the 25th, although we felt it wise that the walks around the donkeys' fields should remain closed for the time being.

June

With her leg in plaster June was almost totally bedridden, and she was rather depressed when she learned that, in view of her age and the probable weakness in her ankle in the future, the Trustees felt that her overseas work should be greatly reduced. They agreed, though, that as she had been responsible for setting up the Indian project, she should continue her work there. I was managing to care for June quite adequately – until the 23rd of June! I was feeding the birds in my aviary that morning when my foot turned over on an uneven patch of ground and, to my horror, I heard a distinct cracking noise. I managed to finish what I was doing and I limped into June's room. Sitting down heavily on a chair, I took off my sock and shoe to find that my ankle had swollen to twice its normal size. June phoned Andrew immediately, who brought X-ray equipment from the donkey hospital! The resulting X-ray was inconclusive so, despite my protests, they insisted that I should be taken to the local hospital. The doctor decided there was a small fracture and I was put in plaster. What a pair June and I were – only two good legs between us! While June's was the left leg, mine was the right, and we felt there must be some way we could drive a car, although I'm still trying to work that one out.

I thought desperately about how we were going to cope, but my nephew, Peter, sprang to the rescue. I phoned to tell him of our misfortunes and, bless him, as he was between jobs at the time, he was able to come down from Yorkshire immediately to look after us. I can't tell you how much it meant to have Peter there – he was absolutely brilliant. During his years as a hotelier he'd trained as a chef, and he served up the most delicious meals we'd had for ages!. He took good care of us and was such good company.

Vron Millar, the Poitou donkeys' special carer, has looked after them for years, and if it had not been for her trained eye we could have lost Dominique. Vron noticed that Dominique was not joining in the games and was becoming dull, depressed and was losing her appetite. Vron called the vets, who immediately realised Dominique was a very poorly

Dominique.

donkey – her large intestine had twisted and we were facing a life-threatening situation.

Wonderful as our facilities are, Dominique is the size of a large pony, and we knew we would need highly specialised equipment to deal with such a serious problem. A call to The Langford Trust for Animal Health and Welfare, part of the University of Bristol, resulted in an emergency journey in our donkey lorry, with Dominique already under sedation, accompanied by her best donkey friend, Pauline. Dominique had her operation immediately on arrival, and it was a great success!

In her stable with Pauline, Dominique began her recuperation, but it was soon apparent that she had lost her appetite. Having received regular reports on her condition, I guessed that she was missing Vron, so I offered Vron the cost of accommodation close to the Langford Trust and asked if she would be prepared to visit Dominique on a daily basis. Within hours, Vron was on her way to Bristol, and her reunion with the two donkeys was a very emotional moment! Vron didn't take up the offer of accommodation. She took a sleeping bag and slept in the stable, giving Dominique small handfuls of food every hour, night and day –

and her devotion did the trick! Twelve days after the operation Dominique was declared fit to come home.

Many of our donkeys have been with us since the early days and are now very elderly, so I'm afraid we lose donkeys quite regularly. Of course some die as a result of ill health that started before their arrival at the Sanctuary. Post mortems are carried out to broaden our knowledge on the causes of donkey deaths as well as establishing how some very elderly donkeys have been able to live for so long. The Veterinary Investigation Centre at Starcross near Dawlish used to carry out the post mortems for us, but we were advised last year that this could not continue. The work on pathology was being restricted to farm animals and, although they would undertake post mortems if there was a zoonotic link (a disease that could be transmitted to humans), they would not be able to cope with our usual requirements. Because of this our vets would have to play a more important role in donkey

Bill Jordan opening the pathology laboratory.

pathology, and we decided to set up a pathology laboratory at the Sanctuary, with our new vet, Nick Bell, undertaking most of the post mortems. Planning approval was obtained to convert an existing building at Brookfield Farm and, when the building work was completed, the lab was fitted with the necessary pathology equipment. Following our Trustees meeting on 26th June, Bill Jordan did us the honour of performing the official opening ceremony, followed by a tour of the facilities for the Trustees and other guests.

Whilst looking around the facilities Steve Springford had been watching the donkeys in the yard through one of the laboratory windows. He commented to me that the donkeys at Paccombe Farm had looked so much happier than those at Brookfield due to the fact that their yards were covered. We were in the process of covering the yards at Woods Farm this year, with Town Barton Farm being the next on the list. Unfortunately the donkeys at Brookfield would have to wait a little longer. I felt, though, that Steve had proved the case for this enormous undertaking on our farms.

I was delighted to be asked by the RSPCA if I would accept The Lord Erskine Award for my work with animals! It was quite a shock, but a very welcome boost for the Donkey Sanctuary. On 29th June, Peter drove me to Newport in South Wales to receive the award at the RSPCA's Annual General Meeting. I was presented with a lovely engraved glass plaque and a citation. It was quite a job balancing on one leg to receive the award and I felt quite emotional when I spoke a few words of thanks, pointing out that rewards rarely come in the way of humble donkey work! The citation read:

'Dr Elisabeth Svendsen founded the Donkey Sanctuary in 1969 with the aim of preventing cruelty and suffering among donkeys. It is now the largest sanctuary for donkeys in the world.

'In 1976 she founded the International Donkey Protection Trust, improving conditions for donkeys abroad by providing free treatment and educating their owners on donkey care. She also played a key role in setting up the Companion Animal Welfare Council.

'In 1989 she formed the Elisabeth Svendsen Trust for Children and Donkeys (incorporating the Slade Centre charity in 1997) providing riding facilities for children with special needs and disabilities.

'Dr Svendsen has always worked closely with the RSPCA, helping the Society remove donkeys from unsuitable conditions; helping out

The Lord Erskine Award.

with treatment, giving advice when requested and supporting prosecution work. The Donkey Sanctuary assists RSPCA Trainee Inspectors by organising courses in donkey care. RSPCA junior groups are always welcome as are RSPCA members and supporters.

'Jonathan Silk, the RSPCA South West Regional Manager, has personally had dealings with the Donkey Sanctuary for over 25 years, recalling assistance Dr Svendsen gave him with a cruelty case early in his career involving two badly neglected donkeys, Hansel and Gretel. His view is that the Donkey Sanctuary has almost stopped donkey cruelty in this country. They never refuse admission to any donkey and thousands of donkeys are being kept by the Sanctuary, to the highest possible standard of care.

'A visit to the Donkey Sanctuary's main farm and headquarters at Sidmouth is an absolute joy and to be able to witness animals, some of whom have been very badly neglected, living out their lives in such ideal conditions is an experience recommended to all.'

July

By the beginning of July I felt I could cope around the house again, despite still having to use crutches. Peter was able to return to home to continue his search for employment as a hotel manager. June and I missed him and his delicious meals enormously!

This year the EST Centre in Birmingham had been chosen for the venue of the annual Festival and the well known broadcaster Nick Owen opened the proceedings. We were amazed by the enormous number of people who turned up. Although Sutton Park is usually bustling on a Sunday, on this particular day it was full to bursting, and over £11,000 was raised for EST. Unfortunately I was still on crutches, which curtailed my activities somewhat, but I was installed in the marquee and spent most of the day signing my books.

Executives' meetings are held in my office on most Tuesday mornings, when we have the opportunity to up-date each other on what is happening in each department. It's a great team, which contributes well to the efficient running of the charity. In common with other charities, a five-year strategic plan has been established and much of the executives' time is spent in ensuring that we are moving forward as planned. There are so many aspects to take into account as the Donkey Sanctuary has grown so large, but it is hard to predict the future when we never know how many donkeys will be coming into our care. Reports from our team of Welfare Officers, whose job it is to regularly visit foster homes and give advice if needed, as well as following up reports of cruelty to donkeys or neglect, were indicating that we now had an excellent knowledge of the donkey population in the UK.

August

Apart from donkeys used for donkey derbies, nowadays the only working donkeys in the UK are those giving rides to children on the beaches. Bill Tetlow, our Regional Welfare Officer for the North of England, Scotland and Northern Ireland has always had a special interest in these donkeys. With Blackpool Borough Council, he came up with the idea of awarding 'Donkey Oscars' to the best kept donkeys on the beaches at Blackpool. The award scheme was to include a monthly presentation of rosettes, and an end-of-year award ceremony with a trophy for the overall winner. I willingly agreed to join Bill in Blackpool to assist with judging at the first inspection but I have to admit I hadn't realised how far it was between the North and South Piers. Every week, the donkey operators move to a different 'stand'

Presentation of the Donkey Oscars on Blackpool beach.

between the piers so that they all have the opportunity to work at the more popular spots and experience the vagaries of tide-tables. Although I was no longer using crutches, my ankle was aching badly by the end of the day, but I was pleased to see how well the donkeys were cared for and how keen their owners were to receive a 'Donkey Oscar'.

Bill gives regular talks on our work to various groups and organisations in his area. During our visit to Blackpool he showed me a poster advertising a talk he was due to give in the near future, and I was amused to see the title – 'Working for Wonder Woman'! It has been a source of amusement to us both ever since, as he continues to tease me about it!

As the EST Festival was not held in Sidmouth this year we decided to hold a 'Fun Day' instead, and I think it was one of the most successful events we'd ever held. The day was made very special by the guest appearance of Dame Thora Hird. Thora was accompanied by a film crew recording a BBC television programme, 'Arena', about her life. By the time she arrived in our car park not only were a donkey and cart waiting to take her to the main arena, but a large crowd had also gathered. Immediately Thora regaled the crowd with delightful

Dame Thora Hird, star of our Fun Day.

stories, and we had quite a job to make a clear way for her triumphant entry into the main field! She was cheered all the way by ever-increasing crowds, as cars poured into our free car parks. Once again, no charge was made for entry to the Fun Day and parents and children were able to enjoy a real family day out.

Thora took the microphone to open the 'Handy Donkey' display and, once again, she entertained the thousands present with her wonderful anecdotes! After watching the display, Thora joined me where I was signing books in the EST Centre arena. You should have seen the crowds there, all wanting Thora's autograph, delighted to talk to her or even just to touch her. We even had to become crowd controllers, just to give Thora some air! We then made a quick visit to the donkey hospital where our Director of Veterinary Services, Andrew Trawford, was able to show Thora the donkeys in our intensive care unit. She was particularly interested to see Pussy Willow, who was just recovering from a very complicated operation for colic, successfully performed by Alex Thiemann, assisted by Vicky Grove, two of our five vets.

After lunch in the Hayloft restaurant, Thora, still surrounded by crowds, returned to the outdoor arena to watch the EST children perform a pantomime called 'The Donkey's Dream' which she really enjoyed. We had a car waiting by the arena and, amid tumultuous cheers, Thora climbed into the car to be taken back to London by Ian Humphries, one of our drivers.

On the day we raised almost £10,000 for the charity, and we were so grateful to all those who volunteered to help us and, of course, our magnificent staff. Bob Venn, the new Principal of EST Sidmouth, had really been thrown in at the deep end in having to organise everything, and I lost no time in congratulating him.

September

I'd received a request to give a talk to the Danish Donkey Breed Society at the home of one of their members which, by pure coincidence, was only ten miles from Randers, where Lise lives. As I was planning to visit her during the summer I was able to combine the two. The talk proved quite difficult. After only a couple of minutes I realised that the faces of most of my forty-strong audience were completely blank. When I asked how many of them spoke English only five people stood up, and I was somewhat disconcerted at having to pause regularly during my talk so that Lise could translate for me. The talk went down well, however, and everyone seemed to enjoy it. Afterwards Lise and I visited

Farno, a little island near Esberg where I was to catch the ferry home, and we had a wonderful time scouring the beach for the pieces of amber that are regularly washed up on the shore. Lise seemed to find much more than me but between us we found a fair amount, although they were nothing compared to the large pieces that are seen in jewellery shops.

Press and media attention was increasing all the time, thanks mainly to Dawn's enthusiasm in issuing regular press releases to encourage more interest in our work. Articles were appearing in the *Daily Mail*, the *Mail on Sunday*, the *Sunday Independent*, *Western Daily Press* and many local newspapers throughout the UK. Various magazines featured the Donkey Sanctuary, too, the most unusual of which was *Scania* magazine. The article, quite naturally, centred around our Scania lorry with its custom-built donkey-box body! During the year we had also been featured in the local BBC programme, 'Spotlight', and, of course, the Channel 4 programme, 'Pet Rescue'.

For a long time I had been promising Clive and Grainne that I would visit them and their son, Sam, at their new home in the USA, and I was able to use the tickets awarded to me by Virgin Atlantic following the flight problems in March. The family had moved to Madison in Wisconsin in at the beginning of the year. Clive had been appointed as a Professor at the University of Wisconsin-Madison and had his own research unit there doing intensive research on Parkinson's disease and motor neurone disease. This involves generating stem cells in the laboratory and transplanting them to try to replace dying cells in the brain.

Sadly, I chose a very bad time to go. I flew to New York on 7th September, stayed overnight and the following afternoon I flew to Madison. The plane flew over Manhattan, giving a magnificent view of the twin towers of the World Trade Centre. My fellow passengers and I remarked on how beautiful they looked, bathed in the late afternoon sunshine. It was lovely to see Clive and his family again and catch up on all the news. On the morning of 11th September I walked to the local supermarket and was surprised when I walked in to find all the shoppers standing quietly in the aisles, listening intently to a voice coming over the public address system. I thought this was rather unusual, so I stopped to listen to what was being said. Like everyone else I was absolutely horrified to hear of the events that were unfolding in New York and Washington. I lost all interest in shopping and rushed back to Clive's house where Grainne had just returned home from her voluntary work. For the rest of the day we sat watching the television in a state of shock.

My planned return home via New York two days later wasn't possible, so I remained with Clive and his family for a few extra days until I was able to book a direct flight from Chicago to London. As we approached the airport my taxi driver said he'd never seen O'Hare International Airport so empty; only the terminal dealing with the flight to the UK was open, and the plane was almost empty.

Due to the cancellation of my return flight Virgin Atlantic offered me free return standard flight tickets for two people, which had to be used within twelve months. However, by this time I'd had enough, and I decided to offer them to the staff by way of a draw. I was delighted when Ray and Julie Mutter won, and they took a well-earned break to St Lucia.

October

This month we had a royal visitor to the Sanctuary. His Royal Highness, Prince Laurent of Belgium, had founded his own charity, the Prince

A royal visit.

Laurent Foundation, which was dedicated to the cause of animal welfare. He wanted to present me personally with an award in recognition of the 'extraordinary' work I had undertaken and the Donkey Sanctuary's devotion to the cause of donkeys. The Prince arrived with a party of 29 members of his charity and various members of the Belgian press. We were pleased to show everyone around our facilities, including the Slade Centre where the award, a lovely bronze statue, was presented to me.

We had arranged to have a royal lunch at the 'Hayloft', although this was somewhat delayed as, still full of energy, Prince Laurent decided to take a stroll down to the sea. As some of you may know, the sea is about one-and-a-half miles away down a footpath that is very steep and slippery in places, and the return journey feels more like five miles! Although the Prince had set off with a large number of his retinue, one by one they returned to the Sanctuary, out of breath and completely exhausted! We were all relieved when the Prince himself returned, face glowing from the fresh air and ready for lunch! After lunch I was pleased to present him with a Donkey Sanctuary sweatshirt as well as a baseball cap which he wore for the remainder of his visit!

November

Over the last few years I have had regular correspondence with a charming American lady, and we have become good friends. She usually visits the Sanctuary twice a year, accompanied by her companion, and she has always contributed very generously to both our charities. I was overwhelmed when she came to see me in November and offered a donation of $1 million dollars! This magnificent gift was to be divided so that the Donkey Sanctuary would receive two-thirds, with the remainder for EST. I was very close to tears when I realised that yet another of my dreams was going to come true – the boost to EST's funds would go a long way towards the costs of building a fourth Centre. I can never thank this lady enough for the help she has given us.

Dame Thora Hird and I had become firm friends over the last few years, and we kept in close contact, but my thoughts had been turning to how I could repay her for the marvellous support she had given to us. Special appearances of celebrities usually involve the payment of a fee, but Thora had never charged us a penny. Having discussed this with Lord Soulsby, he agreed to host a tour of the House of Lords, which would include lunch in the Peers Dining Room. I booked a taxi to collect Thora from her home, and she was absolutely thrilled with her day, saying it was one of the best she'd ever had!

In late November I was proud to take part in a ceremony at the University of Glasgow when Dr Feseha Gebreab, our Ethiopian project leader, was bestowed with an honorary degree. It was good to meet up with old friends again, and I had the opportunity to discuss my forthcoming opening lecture at the BEVA Congress with Sandy Love. I resolved that, on my return to Devon, I would start preparing what I was going to say, as it had to be ready for publication in the *Veterinary Record* and the *Veterinary Times* at least two months before the Congress itself.

December

The final event of the year at the Donkey Sanctuary was our Candlelight Evening. Members of staff in the main office had suggested this idea. For a small donation, supporters could send us dedications which would be attached to lighted candles placed around the Sanctuary. In

The Candlelight Evening.

the event, over 12,000 dedications were received in memory of loved members of family, friends or pets – and indeed for lots of other reasons! On the day, every candle had to be lit! The staff was absolutely wonderful and, despite the bitterly cold weather, managed to light all the candles. This was no mean task, as the wind whistled and blew many of them out as soon as they were lit! Candles had been set out to form the shape of a donkey on the hill opposite the main yard, but, after several attempts to light the candles, this had to be abandoned, and a generator was set up to electrically illuminate the silhouette. In the early evening we held a carol service outside New Barn, and dozens of people turned up. We had planned to sing ten carols, but the weather was so cold, with a wind-chill factor of around -10°, and we only managed five carols before we decided that enough was enough! The donkeys must have been highly amused to see us nearly freezing to death, while they stood in comfort in their nice warm barn! It was a successful event, though – the donations received were well worth the suffering, and we resolved to hold another Candlelight Evening next year – with some modifications to ensure greater comfort!

June and I set off on our Christmas/New Year cruise on the *Aurora* and this year we were engaged in a new interest. There was a pottery class on board, and every day we spent some time making brightly coloured clowns. The end results were really lovely, and I decided that I would auction mine next Donkey Week to raise funds for the charity.

2   0   0   2
ANOTHER DISASTER
ON THE BROADS

January

I am able to attend the majority of my meetings in London by travelling up and back in a day by train from Honiton station. It entails an early start and a late return, but spares the cost of overnight accommodation and I can be back in the office at my usual time of 7.30am the following morning. However, this is not always possible.

Early in the year I decided to meet up again with Victor Watkins. He has been with the World Society for the Protection of Animals (WSPA) for a long time and, over twenty years ago, we had worked together to construct a code of practice for working donkeys in Spain. Since then, part of his remit has been to rescue bears in Turkey from cruel people who, by whatever means they can, make them 'dance' for an unsuspecting public in return for money. It was lovely to meet him again after all these years. WSPA had recently moved to a larger office close to the River Thames in Vauxhall. Taking me to the window to admire the view, Victor pointed out the playing field between the building and the river where terrorists had assembled the missile that had been fired at the MI5 building on the opposite bank. I saw what a clear view was available to the terrorists and felt it was very fortunate that only a minimal amount of damage was done.

On this occasion I was staying overnight at my daughter's home. Sarah and her partner, Paul, had invited me to have dinner with them, Paul's mother Eve and her partner, David, that evening. As far as I was aware this was to be a quiet dinner, but Paul suddenly appeared with a bottle of champagne. I nearly cried with joy when he gave us the wonderful news that Sarah was going to have a baby. As you can imagine, the evening turned into quite a celebration and I was touched to notice how attentive Paul was to Sarah, and how proud they both were!

February

With such a large family of donkeys, many of whom have been with us for years, the care needed for the growing number of elderly donkeys was becoming more and more intensive. Michael Crane, our Senior Veterinary Surgeon, was often away giving lectures to students and vets all over the country. It was agreed, therefore, to employ two more vets to cover the extra workload. As a veterinary Trustee, Bill Jordan was one of the interview panel for prospective candidates, and Tess Sprayson and Honor Duffield joined our team of experts. We also employed Keith Powell on a year's contract to carry out an epidemiological study in Tigray and Amhara – a very necessary expansion of our work in Ethiopia.

Luckily for me, the Sanctuary has a researcher on its staff. Catherine Morriss co-ordinates research within the Sanctuary and with outside bodies; she also manages and arranges training on the veterinary computer system, organises the ragwort campaign and oversees a harnessing project in Kenya. She was able to help me prepare my lecture for the BEVA Congress in September, compiling facts and figures which I was sure would be of interest to the delegates.

Sue Harland and I make many tedious train journeys from Honiton to Waterloo and back. Sue has been with me for many years and is an excellent and efficient PA. Our office is always extremely busy, dealing with an amazing variety of problems and queries relating to the charities. Sue also accompanies me to many of my meetings, and how she manages to take some of the complex minutes I will never know. She also looks after our secretary, Fiona Trim, who is equally talented and has an extremely good memory – invaluable in times of crisis! However, back to our train journeys. Occasionally we meet interesting fellow travellers. On one occasion we bought slices of hot pizza just before we boarded the train and, on entering a carriage, we found just two empty seats next to two gentlemen who were quietly sitting reading their newspapers. Holding our pizzas aloft we asked if we could take the seats. 'Only if we can have some of your pizza!' one of the gentlemen replied. This, of course, broke the ice and we chatted happily on all sorts of subjects including, of course, my work for the donkeys as well as current affairs. Terrorism and the problems with Afghanistan were uppermost in our minds and we were all airing our views on what should be done. On arrival at his station, one of the gentlemen stood up to leave and, as he did so, he handed me his business card and said how much he'd enjoyed our conversation. When we'd settled down again, I glanced at the card, and was somewhat taken aback when I saw that he was a high-ranking member of the Ministry of Defence!

On another occasion Sue and I had spent most of the journey chatting to each other and it wasn't until we were travelling through Dorset that two gentleman in the opposite seats recognised me and we started talking together. We were so engrossed in conversation that they simply forgot to get out of the train at their destination, Axminster! Hasty phone calls to their wives resulted in their travelling on to Honiton station, whereupon they joined us in Sue's car back to the Sanctuary. Within a few moments of our return one of their wives had arrived to collect them.

March

Saturday 2nd March was a disastrous day for me! As usual I spent a couple of hours in the office, after which June and I did our weekly shopping. We enjoyed lunch at our favourite pub, The White Horse, before returning home. The weather was beautiful for the time of year, and I decided to take the dogs out for a walk. With the dogs firmly attached to their leads, I set off down the drive, well in control. Through the gate we went but, just as I turned to shut it again, I was suddenly jerked off my feet as all four dogs decided to give chase to next door's cat! I 'surfed' up the lane on my stomach, desperately holding on to the galloping dogs. It would probably have appeared very amusing to an onlooker, but when I eventually gained control of the dogs I realised how painful my left wrist was. I told the dogs in no uncertain terms that they should forget their afternoon stroll, and returned to the house feeling very much the worse for wear. Since contracting osteomyelitis in my right hand many years ago I am unable to use it properly, and to have an injury to the left hand was quite a blow.

I went to June's room to tell her what had happened. At that stage my wrist didn't look too bad so I decided to go and rest for a while to see if the pain subsided, but within an hour it was obvious that something was wrong, and so off we went to the Casualty Department again! I was told that I had suffered a Colles fracture and my wrist was put in plaster which had to stay on for five weeks.

I'd arranged another family get-together for late March. All the children and grandchildren came, as well as Eve and David. Once again I organised a treasure hunt and, while the family scoured East Devon, June and I organised section 2 of the day's entertainment. Following our success at making clowns on the *Aurora,* we decided that the family should have a go. So, on their return, they were provided with overalls and asked to make models which would be judged and the appropriate points added to their treasure hunt scores.

It would have been difficult for me to cook dinner so, when everyone had finished their tasks we adjourned to the Blue Ball at Sidford, where I had booked a private room for dinner and presentation of the prizes. One team was the outstanding winner – the Danish team.

The family's models.

I was interested to learn from a lady named Mrs Fuller that a plaque had been erected in Covent Garden in memory of 100,000 costermongers' donkeys who had worked in and around the market from 1661 to 1974. Mrs Fuller sent me a photograph of the plaque and some photos of Derby George, the donkey used as the model for the plaque, surrounded by 'pearlies' representing the era in which the donkeys had been working. What a lovely idea.

April

I often have to sign up to fifty letters a day and, having problems with both wrists, I was finding work very difficult, so I was relieved when the plaster was removed from my wrist on 3rd April. June and I decided that we would spend a week on the Norfolk Broads to rest and recuperate. A week earlier we had found a new little dog for June at an animal rescue centre to replace her dachshund, Zara, who had died a few months previously. Tilly was a Yorkshire/Tibetan terrier-cross and, because June didn't want to waste 'bonding time' with her new charge, we decided that she should join us. So we set off on 5th April, with June driving and Tilly curled up comfortably on my lap.

My nephew, Peter, was now manager of the Butterfly Hotel at Bury St Edmunds, and June and I spent our first night with him, enjoying a lovely dinner and chatting about old times. We continued our journey early on Saturday morning, having invited Peter to join us on our boat for the weekend. Being aware of our previous adventures on the Broads perhaps he should have known better than to accept!

We stopped to do some shopping just before we reached our destination, and had unpacked and settled on the boat before Peter arrived at 2.30pm. After welcoming him on board, I decided to go for a short walk down a lane alongside Hickling Broad and, as June still had a few chores to do, she happily agreed that I should take Tilly with me. I was savouring the thought of a whole week of total rest and relaxation. As I walked, I spotted a man in his garden accompanied by a large golden retriever. The dog spied Tilly and it came thundering towards us. The man saw what was happening and was desperately shouting at the dog to stop, but it continued to charge straight toward us. I swiftly grabbed Tilly up into my arms to protect her, and the dog ran straight into me, throwing me across the lane where I landed in a heap on the ground. To my horror I could see immediately that my left foot was bent the wrong way and I could see bone just beneath the surface of the skin. I had no choice but to grab my foot firmly and twist it back into the correct position, although I knew by the grinding sound that it was badly broken. The owner of the dog offered me his arm, saying 'You're not hurt – come on, I'll help you up,' but I knew it was out of the question, and told him so. I asked him to call for an ambulance, and that was the last I saw of him! Fortunately there were other people around who came to see if they could help, and someone set off at a run to fetch June and Peter while I sat, still holding onto Tilly. I was absolutely devastated; I could see months of pain and disability ahead of me and, even worse, I felt so sad that my work with my beloved donkeys would be curtailed enormously.

June and Peter arrived just in time to see my ankle being put in a splint by the paramedics and I was carried off in an ambulance to the James Paget Hospital at Gorleston-on-Sea, near Great Yarmouth – the hospital where Pat had been taken when she broke her ankle.

I didn't have to wait long before my ankle was X-rayed and a drip inserted into my arm to control the pain, but I was horrified when the specialist told me that my ankle was so badly damaged he doubted that I would ever walk properly again. He dismissed June's suggestion that a splint could be put back on to enable me to be taken back to Exeter, where June's specialist, Mr Jameson-Evans, might be able to help. He promised he would do the best he could during an operation the next morning. As you can imagine, I was feeling really depressed as I was wheeled into a ward and June and Peter returned to the boat. The ward was so busy, no-one had time to undress me or give me anything to eat until after 11pm. Then I was brought a sandwich and told to eat it quickly, as the operation was booked for early the following morning and I was not supposed to eat anything after midnight! I was awake for most of the night, in pain and worrying about the future, but I must have been dozing at around 8am when I was startled by a voice calling me. 'Dr Svendsen?' asked the gentleman standing by my bed. He looked at me kindly and said, 'You're Dr Svendsen from the Donkey Sanctuary?' I confirmed that I was, and he went on, 'My wife and I owe you a deep debt of gratitude.' I looked at him, not really taking in what he was saying. 'Before coming to Great Yarmouth I worked at the orthopaedic hospital in Exeter for nine years. My daughter, Harriet, attended Ellen Tinkham School in Exeter, which sent Harriet and her little friends to your Centre in Sidmouth to ride the donkeys. Harriet, who has special needs, never showed enthusiasm for anything other than the donkeys, and so she was brought to the Centre twice a week. The proudest day of our lives was when my wife and I watched Harriet being presented with an award for cheerfulness by Captain Sensible at one of your Festivals.' 'I remember,' I said, recalling the fun we'd all had that day. 'I'm Mr Jones, the orthopaedic specialist, and if anybody can make you walk again, Dr Svendsen, I will,' he said. 'I'll see you in the operating theatre. Don't worry.' It was an amazing coincidence, and I realised later how fortunate I had been. Mr Jones was supposed to be off duty that weekend but had been contacted because of the complicated break I'd suffered. He recognised my name and returned to the hospital to operate on my ankle. He told me later that the bones in my foot had been reduced to a 'mush', and my notes read:

'Left ankle trimaleollar fracture; Lateral incision; Very comminuted lateral malleolar fracture with almost no extension above the level of the ankle joint

'No opportunity for any screws in the malleolus itself – therefore 6 hole 1/3 dcp used as a buttress plate – check X-rays satis(factory)

'Medial incision; The medial malleolar fragment appeared initially and superficially to be a single fragment. No such luck! The medial cortex was a shell over a comminuted medial malleolus. Held with 2mm K wire then 2 screws – semithreaded – introduced with washers. Check X-rays satis(factory).'

Following the operation I had to stay in hospital for eleven days. The first plaster had to be removed because of an enormous fracture blister. I was re-plastered the day before I left, and told that it would have to remain in place for nine weeks. June had been absolutely marvellous while I was there, visiting every day, bringing me much-needed clothes and toiletries and occasional tasty snacks. The final instructions from Mr Jones were that I was not to move my foot under any circumstances.

He said the mush of bones had been attached to a metal buttress. Any undue movement could cause them to become detached and nothing further could be done. I realised that I would have to stay in bed until the plaster was removed.

Several months after my accident I received a letter from the owners of the dog that had bowled me over. They explained that they'd only had the dog, called Snowy, for a couple of months and they hadn't had time to train her. They sent me a donation for EST and commiserated on my misfortune.

Whilst in hospital I received the sad news that our dear friend Butch had died. Butch was the 3,383rd donkey to come into our care. His death, however, was balanced by the birth of a handsome little colt foal at the Sanctuary. His mother, Red Rose, who was heavily pregnant, came into our care with five companions after losing their home when a northern-based animal park was closed down. I immediately decided this little foal could be a permanent reminder of the pleasure Butch had given us all for so many years, and he was named 'Little Butch'.

John Pile had removed one of the seats in his car and made up a makeshift bed so that he could collect me from the hospital. His wife, Sheila, who helps me in the house and cares for the animals when June and I are away, had prepared my room and it was such a relief to get home.

May

I was able to continue working from my bed, with the help of a connection to the office phone network and twice-daily visits from Sue. The regular Executives meetings took place in my bedroom! I realised, though, that I wasn't going to be able to put in an appearance at Donkey Week. I was determined to do as the specialist had told me, rather than risk never being able to walk again.

Paul readily agreed to take over my role during Donkey Week, and he did a brilliant job. His first task was to welcome all our visitors to the Sanctuary, aided by a short video of me in my bed, which had been filmed by Dan Bryan.

The clown I had modelled during my cruise was auctioned during the week and raised the amazing amount of £320!

Paul was pleased to introduce Mr Kennedy-Melling to our visitors. In memory of the late actress, Barbara Miller, Mr Kennedy-Melling offered us a lovely trophy to present annually to someone of our choosing in recognition of their exceptional work for the Donkey

Little Butch with his mother, Red Rose.

Sanctuary. We had no doubt who the first recipients should be – Janet and Peter Thorne – for their wonderful work in raising funds for our charities. I felt this would be a lovely way of thanking them. Of course they had absolutely no idea that they were to receive an award and were staggered when their names were called out. It seemed especially appropriate to me, as Peter, who is a farmer, had recently suffered a broken leg and, like me, he'd had to rest for a long period of time, which I knew must have been difficult for such an active person.

I had so many visitors during the week. Mo Flenley always attends Donkey Week and makes additional visits throughout the year, and I was delighted to see her. In the past Mo has been so keen to stay grooming the donkeys all day that she often missed the coach that took everyone back to their hotels in Sidmouth! Nowadays, though, she

Maureen (Mo) Flenley.

remains within walking distance of the Sanctuary, and can be with the donkeys as long as she wishes.

June had to visit India just after Donkey Week, and my care of Pat when she broke her ankle was now repaid, as she came to look after me, bless her! It amused me to think that I'd looked after Pat and June for weeks; June had looked after me – and now Pat was caring for me. What a threesome we were!

June

I did as I was told and stayed in bed for nine weeks, and then I returned to Exeter by ambulance – it was such a relief to have the plaster removed. An X-ray showed that the bones in my ankle were safely in the correct position and Mr Jameson-Evans was very pleased with the results. Of course I still needed to support my ankle as much as possible. Crutches were difficult for me to use as my left wrist was still very weak, so I had to use a zimmer frame around the house and a wheelchair when I went out.

Paul had made several visits to Europe to see what could be done to help the poor donkeys who were being transported across Europe to be slaughtered for meat. These donkeys often crossed many countries, and borders, before arriving at their final destination. Slovenian officials are being very co-operative and the Donkey Sanctuary was hoping to set up a rescue station on the Italian/Slovenian border, so that donkeys who were not fit to travel could be removed from the transporters. Although this has not so far been possible, with our encouragement the Slovenian Government vets have tightened up their rules and few bad cases are now being reported

We were therefore absolutely appalled when we heard that a restaurant in Scotland was serving a ravioli dish containing donkey meat. We were made aware of this by the *Sunday Mail* in Glasgow; when we asked, the restaurant insisted that no cruelty to donkeys was involved. However, this wasn't acceptable to British animal lovers. Paul quickly made public the appalling and unacceptable conditions in which donkeys were being transported thousands of miles across Europe, to be slaughtered for meat. As a result, the owner of the restaurant was inundated with letters and faxes and withdrew his ravioli dish from the menu. Two months later the *Mail on Sunday* revealed that donkey meat sausages were being sold at a delicatessen in an English seaside town and, again, they insisted that no cruelty to donkeys was involved. The sausages were ordinary cuisine in France and didn't cause any offence there. Pressure from the *Mail on Sunday* newspaper, with the backing of the Donkey Sanctuary, forced the restaurant owner to stop selling his sausages.

After nine weeks away from my desk a temporary office was arranged for me in a ground floor meeting room. Every day at 7.30am, John Pile helped me into a wheelchair and took me from the house, entering the office through the French windows that open onto the Russell Garden. The wheelchair was left just outside ready for my return. One day I was surprised when a middle-aged couple tapped on the French windows and came inside. Their question puzzled me. 'Where would a person who should be in a wheelchair be able to walk to?' I said I didn't understand the question, and the gentleman said, pointing to my wheelchair, 'Mother was here a moment ago, and now she's disappeared. She's not fit to walk very far, and we're getting worried. Where can she have gone?' I explained that the wheelchair was mine, and 'mother' must have wheeled herself off to see the donkeys! Poor things – they were so embarrassed.

June accompanied me on one of my visits to see Mr Jameson-Evans. While I was waiting to be called in we chatted with a lady who was also waiting. When the lady realised that we came from Sidmouth she asked us if we knew the Donkey Sanctuary. Before we had time to reply she said, 'I visit the Sanctuary frequently and I know Dr Svendsen very well.' It was a difficult situation and fortunately (or perhaps unfortunately for the lady) the specialist arrived and said to me, 'Dr Svendsen – please come in.' The poor lady must have been so embarrassed!

To begin with I had physiotherapy every third day and, although some of the daily exercises were excruciating, I was determined to persevere to regain maximum use of my ankle. There was no way I would accept not being able to walk again. Visits to the physiotherapist were later reduced to once a week, and I was quite surprised one day when Theresa, the physiotherapist, said to me, 'The next thing we have to do is to get your leg over!' I looked at her in amazement; but she explained that a huge sign of progress for patients with lower limb injuries is when they can go down stairs 'leg over leg' rather than having to step down onto each stair with the strong leg, bringing the other leg after it. I was quite relieved to hear the explanation and delighted when I managed to get my leg over as I left the office each day!

July

The result of our feasibility study to find a site for a fourth EST Centre had clearly favoured Manchester. Debbie and Mark had looked at several sites but none had seemed suitable. At one stage we thought we were going to have to choose another area, but the council then offered to lease us a beautiful site adjacent to a lake in Debdale Park. I was determined to go up to Manchester to look at the site and, in early July, Mark drove us to Manchester. I think he must have been very embarrassed when we stopped for a 'comfort break'! He removed my wheelchair from the back of the car and pushed me into the motorway services. I had no choice but to use the toilet for the disabled, but I'd never had to try pulling open a heavy door towards me while sitting in a wheelchair. It proved nearly impossible, and poor Mark had to come to the rescue, waiting outside to help me in and out. Perhaps I should consider designing an easier way for disabled people to go the toilet!

Joined by Debbie, we went to Debdale Park for a site meeting with council officials. Mark had to push me in my wheelchair, which must have been hard work. Suddenly, I was stopped in mid-sentence as a man who had been standing close by, rushed up to me saying, 'You're Dr Svendsen of the Donkey Sanctuary, aren't you?' Before I could answer, he threw his arms around me and kissed me full on the lips! Then he walked away again. I saw Mark and Debbie giggling behind their hands and, although I wasn't amused at the time, I must admit I could see the funny side of it later. Despite some problems, we decided that the site in Debdale Park would be ideal for the Centre and Mark set about preparing the plans so that planning approval could be sought.

August

Three Gates Farm, under the managership of John Fry, had belonged to the Sanctuary for many years. John and his wife, Monica, cared for many of the early donkey arrivals, with the result that a large percentage of their donkeys were now very elderly and in need of frequent veterinary visits.

We decided to adapt the barns at Trow Farm to give maximum comfort to these geriatric donkeys and to bring them closer to the

Three Gates donkeys happily settled at Trow Farm.

hospital. It was agreed that, over the spring and summer months, the donkeys would be brought back to Trow Farm, and that Three Gates Farm would be sold. All the staff at Three Gates were offered work on one of our farms or given the opportunity to take redundancy which, in the event, the majority did. The last group of donkeys was brought back to Trow Farm in July.

Before my accident I was asked if I would open the Pets n' People Show at Shugborough Hall near Stafford. The organisers, Jane and Tony Kimberley, had very kindly chosen EST to be their charity of the year and EST would benefit from the profits of the show. It was a great success, and I think those present enjoyed my opening talk on that beautifully sunny day. There was plenty to see – Shetlands and other native breeds of ponies, heavy horses, falcons, and the Reverend Graeme Sims and his sheepdog display. I was pleased to see both EST and Donkey Sanctuary staff manning their exhibition stands, and some of the donkeys from the Birmingham Centre were very popular with the visitors. The wonderful donation we received later from Mr and Mrs Kimberley was very much appreciated. Without sponsorship such as this I don't know how we'd manage to keep the Centres operating.

Dawn advised me on my return that *Blue Peter* magazine had decided to adopt Peanuts, the little donkey born with twisted legs. The magazine featured news on Peanuts each month and, as a result, many children have joined 'Donkidz'. *Pony* magazine featured the story of Fortunada, the first donkey rescued in Spain since Blackie Star in 1987. Fortunada was rescued after being attacked by a pack of dogs, and was now living happily at the new Centre in Spain that we were able to use by working with a Spanish charity. Plans to register the Donkey Sanctuary in Spain are currently taking place, and the purchase of a farm with 22 acres of land and stabling for donkeys is due to be completed in July 2003.

We were all delighted when Dame Thora Hird* agreed to attend the EST Festival in Sidmouth this year. Hundreds of people turned up to see her, and she chatted to everyone as she signed copies of her latest book. Rhodri Williams was there too, in his new role as Patron of EST. He gave us tremendous support, taking over the commentary for the events in the arena as well as spending much of the day helping Sue Hudson and her staff to promote the 'adoption scheme'. Rhodri has

* Sadly, Dame Thora Hird passed away in March 2003.

Dame Thora Hird and our new Patron, Rhodri Williams.

become an excellent Patron and I really cannot thank him enough.

The Donkey Breed Society junior members stayed at the Sanctuary for a week during the school summer holidays. Maggie Taylor, a Trustee of EST and Community Fundraising Officer for the Donkey Sanctuary, brings a group of these young, enthusiastic donkey lovers to stay twice a year, and this was the Juniors' 30th visit! Maggie is absolutely marvellous with the children; they all stay in the Slade Centre for the week and Maggie organises all sorts of donkey-related activities for them to do. Many of the children return year after year and, as I like to make sure they leave with a little gift from the Sanctuary, it is sometimes difficult to choose something different each time. I feel that getting youngsters involved in the donkey-work is a great way of educating them in donkey welfare.

September

We've always kept a visitors' book at our Information Centre, where people can make comments on their visits to the Sanctuary. I was interested to read that Joanna and Kevin from Cumbria visited on 2nd September, and Joanne had written, 'Fantastic place to visit, and the donkeys look very contented. Will be back. Boyfriend has proposed to me here and I said yes!' Perhaps their next visit will be during their honeymoon!

Sarah's baby was due on 30th August, but still hadn't arrived during the first week of September, and I was giving my opening address at the BEVA Congress on Thursday the 12th. In addition, the Donkey Sanctuary was holding another CPD meeting at the Weipers Centre the day before the congress, so I was due to set off for Glasgow on the Tuesday 10th. I was becoming extremely anxious that these two important events would coincide – and I was right! Paul rang me with the news at 6.30am on Monday 9th September, and I was, naturally, over the moon that they had a son. Sarah was able to speak to me briefly and when I asked if they'd chosen the baby's name yet, I must admit I was surprised by her answer. She explained that she'd had the baby just before six o'clock that morning while the shipping forecast was being broadcast. The baby had arrived just as the weather in the shipping area of Fisher was being reported, so the name Fisher was chosen. I wasn't keen at first, but on reflection I felt it was a good job the broadcaster had gone past Dogger Bank and hadn't yet reached German Bight! It could have been much worse. I was upset to hear that the birth had been very difficult and Sarah would have to undergo an operation almost immediately to repair internal damage.

Although I was tempted to abandon my opening address at the Congress and rush to London, I realised that Sarah would have to remain in hospital for a few days and I would be of more help to her when she and the baby returned home. Having been invited by the Dean of the Veterinary School and other Professors from the University to lunch following my talk on Thursday, I felt I should at least put in an appearance, as they had always been so kind and helpful to me. I promised Sarah and Paul that I would travel down to London to be with them immediately afterwards.

On Wednesday I had the pleasure of opening the CPD meeting, which was very well attended. Andrew chaired the meeting, and talks were given by Dr Getachew Mulugeta from our Ethiopian project, three of

Opening the BEVA Congress.

our vets – Michael Crane, Nick Bell and Alex Thiemann – and other well known experts within the veterinary profession; it was a very successful day. Before I returned to the hotel that evening I took the opportunity to pop into the main Conference Centre to see where my ordeal would take place the following day. The main Conference room was a huge theatre-like room, with seating for well over 1,000 people. Seeing it didn't calm my nerves at all.

The big day arrived, and I sat nervously through the John Hickman Memorial Lecture given by Dr Noah Cohen from Texas A & M University entitled 'Colic by Numbers'. It was a brilliant lecture and under normal circumstances I would have been completely engrossed. My big moment arrived, and I was introduced by Sandy Love to the 1,400-strong delegates. I started off by saying, 'Good morning, everybody,' to which I got absolutely no response! I tried again. 'Come along, ladies and gentlemen! This is a difficult moment for me and I need your help. *Good morning* ladies and gentlemen!' A roar of 'Good mornings' came back at me, and from that moment on, as I advised them of the Donkey Sanctuary's work, I had their full attention. Sandy Love couldn't have been more delighted as he helped me down from the podium, thanking me for doing such a good job on their behalf. What a relief – it was all over!

I joined everyone for lunch, but left before it finished to catch my plane, and by 7pm I was in the hospital with Sarah, Paul and Fisher! I

The donkeys join the Oxfam campaign.

was, however, rather annoyed that, despite the hospital being quite new and having excellent facilities, it was very short-staffed and the care Sarah was receiving was practically non-existent. I persuaded the doctor to let Sarah go home, where we could take care of her properly, and we were pleased to get her back. Paul's father, Tony, was already staying at the house and was an enormous help in those first busy days, so I returned to Devon happy in the knowledge that all would be well. Fisher was an absolute angel!

On returning to the Sanctuary I was shown copies of the *Veterinary Record* and the *Veterinary Times*, both of which contained reports on the Congress and a photo taken during my opening address. I felt very pleased.

We don't usually allow our donkeys to be used for publicity campaigns but, as we have a project in Mexico, we agreed to support Oxfam's campaign to draw attention to the problems faced by Mexican farmers who receive barely enough to live on or feed their families from the sale of their coffee beans, whilst vast sums of money are made in the City from the coffee market. After a four-week training course, Sam, George, Tiny, Mo, Cindy and Birdie were taken to London, and laden with 'prop' coffee sacks filled with straw, which were only a fraction of the weight they would have been carrying had the sacks been filled with coffee beans. The commuters' day was brightened up as the donkeys walked through the City to the Stock Exchange, where the sacks were unloaded to symbolise the collapse in world coffee prices that has left 25 million families in Mexico and other countries facing ruin. The event brought reality to today's world where commercialism seems to rule.

Charity Finance is a publication which is circulated around finance departments within the charity field, and in the September issue I was delighted to see that the Donkey Sanctuary's accounts were highlighted. The article pointed out the charity's low administration costs and the fact we had achieved first place in the Charities Aid Foundation's top 500 charities table showing that, for every pound spent on advertising, an amount of £15.24 was raised by way of donations. Also highlighted was the fact that the Sanctuary was to establish a trading subsidiary, 'Donkey World Ltd', from 1st October 2002 to deal with its mail order activities.

It was time to visit Clive, Grainne and Sam once again. However, because I still couldn't walk on my ankle, I decided to meet them in New York. I would have needed my wheelchair to tackle the airport transfer for the flight to Madison. By coincidence, my favourite cruise liner, the *Aurora*, was sailing back to Southampton from New York three days later, so June decided she would fly to New York to join me on the cruise back home again.

The family and I had a wonderful three days in New York, staying at a Holiday Inn. It was wonderful to see Sam enjoying himself and to listen to his non-stop enthusiasm for basketball, which he seemed to play so well. During our open-topped bus tour of the city, he nearly fell out with excitement when we saw a basketball game taking place in the street! Apparently this is a frequent occurrence in the USA and streets are closed for the occasion. It was very sad to visit Ground Zero but we all felt we should go and pay our respects to the many people who had died in the terrorist attack.

I boarded the *Aurora* still an invalid in a wheelchair and, as soon as we had settled into our cabins, I booked daily sessions with Dawn, the physiotherapist, in the massage parlour. Dawn was quite amazing. Every morning, after massaging my foot, she made me do exercises and walked up and down corridors with me, showing me how to put my foot down properly. By the end of the cruise I was able to do two laps around the deck of the ship, and to walk off unaided.

Dawn was fascinated by my stories of the Donkey Sanctuary, and she and some of her fellow crew members adopted some of our donkeys. The Captain of the *Aurora* even adopted Oscar at the Birmingham Centre as a present for his wife! I was pleased to meet Angela Rippon on the ship. She was on board as a guest speaker, and I enjoyed our chat about the old days and the wonderful promotion she had given the Sanctuary in one of her television programmes. Angela suggested that I should do a lecture tour on a cruise to promote our two charities, but I have to admit that I prefer to relax and re-charge my batteries while cruising.

As we sailed up Southampton Water in the early morning, I received a fax from the office telling me that a new filly foal had just been born

Kerry-Anne and Aurora.

to a mare, Kerry-Anne, who had come into our care from an animal park in Wigan that had recently been closed. The mare had been named Kerry-Anne in memory of the daughter of one of our supporters who had died suddenly the previous year. A name for the foal was now needed and, in view of the wonderful cruise and the progress I had made on board with my ankle, I decided that she should be called 'Aurora'. On my return to the office I wrote to Captain Walters to tell him of the ship's new namesake!

October

In late October I attended the launch of the first report compiled by the Companion Animal Welfare Council. This was a comprehensive study on the Identification and Registration of Companion Animals. Later that month I met Elliott Morley, MP, at a meeting of the Associate Parliamentary Group for Animal Welfare in the House of Commons and asked him whether it was possible that CAWC could soon be taken over by the government, as this had been the aim from the start. Mr Morley pointed out that the only drawback was the financial implication. Although I understand the problem, I feel sure that at least some of the participating animal welfare organisations will be happy to continue to assist with finance, on the understanding that the council is recognised by the government. I will keep my fingers crossed.

November

During the autumn I became the unfortunate target of a stalker! Following police advice, we engaged the services of a security firm to keep an eye on the Sanctuary as a whole and me in particular. They were certainly efficient. Every morning they were there when I went out to feed the birds, and they kept me under surveillance as I went to and from the office, as well as following me when I left the Sanctuary. It was a most distressing time but I had one amusing moment. One day I had an appointment for an eye test in Sidmouth and, as usual, I drove into the town through a ford across the River Sid. It had been pouring with rain all day and by the time I was ready to return home there was a roaring torrent in the ford. I drove down the ramp and surveyed the water with dismay, but, as my car is quite large and solid, I decided to risk crossing it. Safely across, I was surprised to see in my rear-view mirror, a small car behind me, trying to do the same!

Svend and Fisher.

I was horrified to see it almost disappear under the rushing water, and I waited to see if the driver needed help. The car kept going, though, and eventually made it to the other side, so I continued my journey home. Walking back to the office I was surprised to see the same car parked at the bottom of the drive – and inside was a very wet, bedraggled looking security man! I couldn't believe that he'd followed me in such a small vehicle and he said shakily that it was the worst trip of his life. He'd followed me to the ford and was amazed to see that I was going through. Of course, his duty was to keep me in his sights all the time. He quickly phoned his associate, who told him, 'Where she goes, you must go'! He was very lucky he wasn't swept downstream into the sea!

December

Sarah and Fisher came to stay with me for a few days in December, and it was wonderful to have them both with me. I was sad when they both went home, but I was soon immmersed in preparing for our second Candlelight Evening. Once again it was an amazing success and over 15,000 candles were lit this year! How the staff managed it I'll never know, but the Sanctuary looked like fairyland, lit up with flickering candles as dusk fell. The Carol Service was shorter this year, and it took place in a sectioned-off area in New Barn. The donkeys in the barn really enjoyed themselves, and joined in with the carol singing. Candlelight Evening seems to have become one of the best staff 'get-togethers' we've ever had! With over 300 staff it is quite difficult to keep the 'family' spirit going, and this feeling is, I'm sure, one of the reasons for the Sanctuary's success. Seeing everyone mingling in the yard, helping each other to light the candles, brought a warm glow to my heart.

It was time for our Christmas cruise once again. I was determined to improve my walking whilst on board and, although I was disappointed that Dawn wasn't on the ship this time, Borjan, a physiotherapist from Slovenia, assisted me equally well. He had been physiotherapist to the Slovenian cycling team and what he didn't know about muscles in the ankles, knees and back was not worth knowing. Regular treatment from Borjan worked wonders and by the end of the cruise I was able to do fourteen laps of the deck – three and a half miles!

I had a gift for the Captain of the *Aurora* and, on New Year's Eve, I was able to present him with a framed picture of little Aurora, which he accepted on behalf of the ship. So the year ended with a promise

from Captain Walters that he would visit the Sanctuary in 2003 to meet the ship's namesake.

Our campaign against the cruel use of a donkey in the annual fiesta in Villanueva de la Vera will continue, and we have been encouraged by new legislation in the Extremadura region (where Villanueva is situated) aimed at protecting defenceless animals from cruelty during fiestas.

Occasionally we are criticised by some people who don't fully understand the nature and variety of our work. They envisage us using large amounts of money on a few elderly donkeys that have nothing to do but stand around all day. I always say, 'Why shouldn't they enjoy a peaceful retirement? Just think what they've contributed to donkeys and their owners around the world, and to children with special needs and disadvantages.' If critics had travelled to some of the poorest and remotest parts of the world with me, seeing real poverty and realising that the only thing that keeps a whole family alive is a donkey, perhaps they would think again. To many of the poorest people a donkey is their only means of scraping together any sort of a living – fetching water, going to market with goods and returning with vital food supplies, working in the brick kilns of India and dying from parasites, wounds and overwork at a very early age. The death of a donkey is a disaster to its owner, who sometimes has to deprive his family of food to purchase another. Our work, particularly in freeing the donkey of parasites, treating foot problems and curing the terrible saddle galls and sores caused by ill-fitting harness (and, indeed, fitting suitable harnessing) enables the donkey to live at least another five years – a life-saver for the poorest people in the world. There are approximately 50 million working donkeys out there and we need increasing funds to reach out to as many as we can.

Neither do the critics take into account the work with special needs children. Anyone who has watched a session at one of our Centres cannot help but be impressed. Hyperactive children are quiet for probably the only time in the week, autistic children smile – and some have been motivated to speech. Physically disabled children have achieved movement previously thought impossible – and all because of the humble donkey!

In January 2003 I will be 73 and the Donkey Sanctuary will celebrate its 30th anniversary in March. What a wonderful 30 years it has been! Apart

The presentation to Captain Walters.

from my rather frequent accidents and tummy troubles, I keep in very good health, and I'm always full of energy! I can't remember a time when my life hasn't revolved around donkeys and I hope and pray that I will be able to carry on the work for many more years. If ever anyone had a dream come true, it is me, and, looking back there is nothing in my life I would wish to change. I shall go on fighting for donkeys' rights and for their welfare until the day I die.

APPENDICES

and obvious expertise. I instinctively knew that she would be an ideal Trustee. In the first instance the Trustees met Wendy on a social level, after which they were unanimous in agreeing that she should be invited to join the board.

Professor Stuart Reid - I'd first met Stuart when he was studying for his PhD at the University of Glasgow, and the Donkey Sanctuary had funded his research on sarcoids. His work had an impact not only on donkeys but a spin-off helped cancer research as well. They found that the papillomavirus partially responsible for the sarcoid was related to that found in cervical cancer in women. Stuart's work was so important that he was soon offered a Professorship, and he became the youngest to reach this high academic status. In addition to his veterinary research skills, Stuart is also very 'computer literate'! He has assisted our charities in many ways over the years; he arranged for a team from the IT department to visit the Glasgow Vet School to see how their veterinary computer system worked, and was instrumental in introducing the Sanctuary to the Internet, arranging, in the early stages, for our web pages to be channelled through Glasgow University's internet site.

Mr Steve Springford - Back In 1989 Steve became one of the first Trustees of The Elisabeth Svendsen Trust for Children and Donkeys. Steve had been involved with the Donkey Sanctuary for many years before that and, as a director of a video production company, he had produced one of our early videos. He became a loyal supporter, raising funds by running stalls at EST Festivals. He is now a director of Celador Productions, which produces television programmes such as 'The National Lottery – Winning Lines' and 'Who Wants to be a Millionaire' – you'll see his name on the credits at the end of these programmes. He has also worked with many famous names, including Cliff Richard and Jasper Carrott, and is the proud owner of his own donkeys.

Consultant to the Donkey Sanctuary's Trustees
Mr John Morgan – John was in banking all his working life, and I first met him as the Manager of the National Westminster Bank when we bought the hotel in Ottery St Mary. His sound financial advice and ability to mix socially with all walks of life makes him a good ambassador for the Sanctuary, and he is very highly regarded and respected. John is now retired, and lives with his wife in Torquay.

Solicitors to the Donkey Sanctuary
Mr John Akers of Messrs Mossop & Whitham of Ottery St Mary, Devon
Mr Paul Voller, Messrs Birchams, 1 Dean Farrar Street, London SW1

THE EXECUTIVE TEAM

Chief Executive	Dr Elisabeth Svendsen,MBE
Deputy Chief Executives	Mrs Mal Squance Mr Paul Svendsen
Director of Finance	Mr John Carroll
Director of Veterinary Services	Mr Andrew Trawford
Director of Management Services	Mr Richard Barnes

STAFF DIRECTORY – THE DONKEY SANCTUARY

Dr Svendsen	Administration	Ian Humphreys	Admissions Dept
Sue Harland	Administration	Brian McConnell	Admissions Dept
Fiona Trim	Administration	Penny Dack	Despatch / Trow Farm
Mal Squance	Administration	Glynis Down	Despatch / Trow Farm
Sue Gooding	Administration	Jan Potbury	Despatch / Trow Farm
Zoë Norris	Administration	Uschi Svendsen	Despatch / Trow Farm
Jacqueline Gosden	Fundraising	Martin Taggart	Welfare Dept
Marian Gumbrell	Fundraising	Tina Court	Welfare Dept
Maggie Taylor	Fundraising	Maxine Carter	Welfare Dept
Danny Bryan	Graphics	Annie Corbin	Welfare Dept
Barry Muir	Graphics	Tessa Anderson	Welfare Dept – AWO
Mark Taylor	Graphics	Alison Barton	Welfare Dept – AWO
Joe Anzuino	Overseas	Carol Bate	Welfare Dept – AWO
June Evers	Overseas	Dawn Brookes	Welfare Dept – AWO
Rob Nichols	Overseas	Jane Bruce	Welfare Dept – AWO
Keith Powell	Overseas	Jillian Bulkley	Welfare Dept – AWO
Paul Svendsen	Administration	Michelle Cargill	Welfare Dept – AWO
Emma Woodward	Administration	Jill Coupe	Welfare Dept – AWO
David Barbour	Farms Administration	Julie Crane	Welfare Dept – AWO
Nigel Blackmore	Farms Admin - Fencing	Wendy Deane	Welfare Dept – AWO
Paul Carter	Farms Administration	Elizabeth Ellis	Welfare Dept – AWO
Suzanne Daly	Farms Administration	Lionel Ford	Welfare Dept – RWO
Annie Hamer	Farms Administration	William Frazer	Welfare Dept – AWO
Jacqui Moss	Farms Administration	Gina Griffin	Welfare Dept – AWO
Tony Waldron	Farms Admin – Fencing	David Harbage	Welfare Dept – AWO
Kay Allen	Management Services	Claire Harper	Welfare Dept – AWO
Tansi Ash	Management Services	Mark Kerr	Welfare Dept – RWO
Richard Barnes	Management Services	Niels Kristensen	Welfare Dept – AWO
Andrea Carroll	Management Services	Jane Lamming	Welfare Dept – AWO
Sue Cockayne	Management Services	Molly Lloyd	Welfare Dept – RWO
Pauline Denning	Management Services	Marie McCormack	Welfare Dept – AWO
Dawn Svendsen	Management Services	Iraina McGroarty	Welfare Dept – AWO
Michael Viksna	Management Services	Pam Moon	Welfare Dept – AWO
Carole Allen	Admissions Dept	Darren Moss	Welfare Dept – AWO
Robbie Bricknell	Admissions Dept	Linda Nield	Welfare Dept – AWO
Vanessa O'Brien	Admissions Dept	Rosemary Pascall	Welfare Dept – AWO

Name	Department	Name	Department
Joanne Pick	Welfare Dept – AWO	Stuart Ford	Buildings/Maintenance Dept
Lynda Rowe	Welfare Dept – AWO		
Trevor Smitheram	Welfare Dept – AWO	Chris Hunt	Buildings/Maintenance Dept
Shelagh Steel	Welfare Dept – RWO		
Bill Tetlow	Welfare Dept – RWO	Peter Newton	Buildings/Maintenance Dept
Penelope Tobin	Welfare Dept – AWO		
Margaret Wallace	Welfare Dept – AWO	David Pavey	Buildings/Maintenance Dept
Tamlin Watson	Welfare Dept – AWO		
Elizabeth Wright	Welfare Dept – AWO	Peter Thomas	Buildings/Maintenance Dept
John Carroll	Accounts Dept		
Tony Anslow	Accounts Dept	Mark Thomson	Buildings/Maintenance Dept
Gerard Bain	Accounts Dept		
Janet Baker	Accounts Dept	Richard Trim	Buildings/Maintenance Dept
Heather Brown	Accounts Dept		
Theresa Conway	Accounts Dept	Rob Waldron	Buildings/Maintenance Dept
Brian Hastie	Accounts Dept		
Sara Whelan	Accounts Dept	Ivan West	Buildings/Maintenance Dept
Judy Woolley	Accounts Dept		
Vanessa Trude	Legacy Dept	Ian Westlake	Buildings/Maintenance Dept
Marie Wilson	Legacy Dept		
David Illsley	Computer Dept	Tim Mason	Gardening Dept
Andrew Brinsford	Computer Dept	Adam Bird	Gardening Dept
Janet Bristow	Computer Dept	William Morley	
Mark Hull	Computer Dept	Martin	Gardening Dept
Tony Munday	Computer Dept	Glen Gardiner	Isolation
James Wellington	Computer Dept	Chris Pile	Isolation
Andrew Trawford	Overseas /Veterinary Dept	Chris Smallacombe	Isolation
		Lisa Spence	Isolation
Margaret Farrow	Overseas /Veterinary Dept	Andrew Judge	Main Yard
		Ami Baker	Main Yard
Dean Hancock	Information Centre	Charlene Cooling	Main Yard
Ellenor Baker	Information Centre	Sharon Cordwell	Main Yard
Wendy Blackledge	Information Centre	Kim Jackson	Main Yard
Margaret Jee	Information Centre	Philip Paver	Main Yard
Sue Squires	Information Centre	Georgina Steed	Main Yard
Judith Tabb	Information Centre	Patsie Walker	Main Yard
Annette Middleton	Main Office	Margaret Warren	Main Yard
Jos Biggs	Main Office	Teresa Jackson	Main Yard – Trow
Amy Carroll	Main Office	Charlotte Pardon	Main Yard – Trow
Sheena Evans	Main Office	Flynte Van-Der-Meulen	Main Yard – Trow
Linda Furzey	Main Office		
Heather Hancock	Main Office	Carol Hounsell	Main Yard – Garmston
Christine Nichols	Main Office	Ben Kennett	Main Yard – Garmston
Angela Norris	Main Office	Sara – Jayne Blair	Main Yard – Hurfords
Linda Popple	Main Office	James Causley	Main Yard – Hurfords
Lorraine Scott	Main Office	Tamsin Dourof	Main Yard – Hurfords
Fiona Shepherd Warren	Main Office	Kelly Gibbs	Main Yard – Hurfords
Alison Stephens	Main Office	David Lee	Main Yard – Hurfords
Sarah Woodward	Main Office	Alan Brown	Trow Farm
Peter Arbury	Buildings/Maintenance Dept	Guy Hucker	Trow Farm
		Gordon Pack	Trow Farm
James Arbury	Buildings/Maintenance Dept	Brian Warren	Trow Farm
		Paul Rockey	Trow Stores

Amanda Gordon	Trow Stores
Sarah Legg	Trow Stores
Tony Squire	Trow Stores
John Pile	Weston
Vron Millar	Weston – Buffalo Barn
Rick Hastie	Weston
Tat Hooper	Weston
Sandra Little	Weston
Jamie Pile	Weston
Chris Rabjohns	Weston
Sandra Somers	Weston
Michael Crane	Veterinary Dept
Dawn Butt	Veterinary Dept
Katherine Cooper	Veterinary Dept
Sue Dabinett	Veterinary Dept
Catherine Morriss	Veterinary Dept
Honor Duffield	Veterinary Dept
Lyssa England	Veterinary Dept
Jane Fleming	Veterinary Dept
Lee Gosden	Veterinary Dept
Vicky Grove	Veterinary Dept
Trudi Hartnell	Veterinary Dept
Paul Phillips	Veterinary Dept
Lorraine Pinn	Veterinary Dept
Joan Rogers	Veterinary Dept
Kate Selley	Veterinary Dept
Tess Sprayson	Veterinary Dept
Esther Stamp	Veterinary Dept
Alex Thiemann	Veterinary Dept
Hayley Trask	Veterinary Dept
Steve Stone	East Axnoller Farm
John Axe	East Axnoller Farm
Peter Daubney	East Axnoller Farm
Janet Doran	East Axnoller Farm
Roy Gudge	East Axnoller Farm
Hayley McConnachie	East Axnoller Farm
Nicola Rabbetts	East Axnoller Farm
Lea Seward	East Axnoller Farm
Sharon Strawbridge	East Axnoller Farm
Malcolm Salter	Brookfield Farm
Herbert Churchill	Brookfield Farm
Judi Davidson	Brookfield Farm
Tony Down	Brookfield Farm
Sue Letheren	Brookfield Farm
Claire Light	Brookfield Farm
Natalie Smith	Brookfield Farm
Sue Solman	Brookfield Farm
Terry Paget	Brookfield Farm-Mechanic
Ian Cottrell	Brookfield Fabrication Workshop
Nigel Cross	Brookfield Fabrication Workshop
David Philcox	Brookfield Fabrication Workshop
Robert Buckland	Vet Dept / Path. Lab
Sophie Cunnington	Vet Dept / Path. Lab
Sarah Norcombe	Vet Dept / Path. Lab
Valerie Patrick	Vet Dept / Path. Lab
Gareth Pinn	Vet Dept / Path. Lab
Wendy Waldron	Printing Dept
Ray Mutter	Newton Farm
Tracey Hall	Newton Farm
Julie Mutter	Newton Farm
David Whetton	Newton Farm
Michelle Yates	Newton Farm
Neil Coles	Paccombe Farm
Richard Beardshall	Paccombe Farm
Donald Churchill	Paccombe Farm
Angharad Hopkins	Paccombe Farm
Sharon McConnell	Paccombe Farm
Janie McDonald	Paccombe Farm
Rosie Nelson	Paccombe Farm
Tracy Payne	Paccombe Farm
Lisa Preatoni	Paccombe Farm
Ron Taylor	Paccombe Farm
Ben Hart	Paccombe Training Centre
Carol Coppin	Paccombe Training Centre
Tracy Highet	Paccombe Training Centre
Liz Hodges	Paccombe Training Centre
Canny Judge	Paccombe Training Centre
Jane Keown	Paccombe Training Centre
David Kingwell	Paccombe Training Centre
Sarah Morrish	Paccombe Training Centre
Laila Tucker	Paccombe Training Centre
Peter Webber	Paccombe Training Centre
Judy Welsman	Paccombe Training Centre
Tracey Philcox	Paccombe Training Centre
Emma Rawling	Town Barton Farm
Rosemary Bowring	Town Barton Farm
Claire Budd	Town Barton Farm
Helen Cleverton	Town Barton Farm
Jill Cocker	Town Barton Farm
Samantha Dawe	Town Barton Farm
Kieran Denman	Town Barton Farm

TRUSTEES OF THE ELISABETH SVENDSEN TRUST FOR CHILDREN AND DONKEYS (EST) AT 1ST JANUARY 2003

Dr Elisabeth Svendsen - Trustee and Honorary Administrator

Mrs Pat Feather - Pat is Dr Svendsen's sister, and was born in Halifax in 1926. She obtained an education degree and taught at several primary schools in Yorkshire. She married in 1949 and has two sons, Peter and Michael. Sadly, her husband, who had served on aircraft carriers during the Second World War, died in 1976, and when Pat felt it necessary to change direction in her life she became the first Principal of The Slade Centre. The work with donkeys and children was a unique experience at the time, and Pat found it was fulfilling to see the success and growth of the project over the years until her retirement in August 1992. As a Trustee of EST, Pat is pleased to be able to play a role in the development of the charity.

Mr R. George Hopkins – George was born in Gloucester in 1930. He attended the Crypt Grammar School, where he became Captain of the hockey and rugby teams, and he played for the Gloucestershire 18+ Schoolboys XV. After National Service in the RAMC George joined a local Farm and Garden Seed Merchants, but left in 1959 for teacher training at Caerleon College. He taught Rural Science in Cwmbran and Southampton, with a further year's training in Rural Science at the City of Worcester College in between. After Southampton he moved into Special Education, working at Stroud, Boreham Wood and, finally, Honiton in 1974 as Headmaster of Mill Water School. During this time he studied at Redland College in Bristol for a Certificate in Special Education, and then with the Open University for a BA degree, which he received in 1979. George retired in 1988.

Mill Water School is where the concept of riding donkeys as therapy for children with special needs arose, and this led to the opening of the Slade Centre. George has been a Trustee since its inception and is now also a Director of the recently formed trading company, Donkey World Ltd. He is also a Trustee of the Otter Value One to One Charity which works with children and adults with hearing difficulties, and is a member of Honiton Rotary Club, being their President in 1983/84. In his spare time he plays tennis, sings with a local group and works in his fairly large garden.

Mr David Miller – After leaving his Methodist boarding school, David joined the RAF where, after a year in the RAF School of Music, he spent four years as a percussion player in the Central Band of the Royal Air Force based in Uxbridge. During this time he participated in many State occasions, including playing in the Guard of Honour outside Buckingham Palace on Coronation Day. He left the Air Force in 1955 and commenced a two-year teacher training course at Trent Park. He worked for seven years in junior schools in Islington, at which point he decided to change direction, obtaining a trainee post in the Children's Department in Southwark. This required a further two years training, at the end of which he became a qualified Social Worker.

In 1972 David moved to Devon, and he worked for Devon County Council Social Services until he retired in 1997. It was in the early 1970s, as part of his work as a Community Development Officer, that he became involved in the establishment of the Slade Centre and became a Trustee.

Mrs Maggie Taylor – Maggie has been a donkey owner for over 30 years. She has four donkeys at present, including two foster donkeys from the Donkey Sanctuary. Maggie has been a member of the Donkey Breed Society since 1969, past member of the Welfare Committee, and chairman of the Junior Committee. For the last 16 years Maggie has run two camps a year at the Sanctuary for Junior DBS members. She is a DBS Award Tester, and has been a volunteer speaker and fund raiser for the Donkey Sanctuary for 20 years. She is currently Community Fundraising Officer, mainly giving talks on awareness.

STAFF DIRECTORY – THE ELISABETH SVENDSEN TRUST FOR CHILDREN AND DONKEYS

VOLUNTARY HELPERS AT THE EST CENTRES

Leeds Centre:

Margaret Arnett
Bryony Bell
David Brooker
Anne Brown
David Cottam
Richard Fryer
Betty Hare
Doreen Haupe
Marilyn Horton
Anne Mathers
Judith Radcliffe
Debbie Walker
Sally Wilkinson

Linda Atkinson
Angela Bickford-Smith
Kathryn Brown
Graham Cocker
Patricia Donaldson
Joel Gaunt
Tricia Harris
Cam Horncastle
Joan Lindsey
Kath O'Shaughnessey
Doreen Swain
Patricia Wheeler
Sue Wood

Avril Bell
Hilary Blundell
Alan Brown
Anne Cooper
Marie Ellis
Roy Hare
Heloise Hartley
Claire Horncastle
Amand Marker
Margaret O'Shaughnessey
Nancy Walcka
Jean White
Audrey Young

PERSONNEL WORKING ON OUR OVERSEAS PROJECTS

INDIA

Dr Vijo Varghese
Dr G. Murugan
Kailash Kuamr
Mr Ajay

Dr Ramesh Kumar
Mr K. J. Joseph
Mr Umpal

Dr Suchitra Balakrishnan
Rajinder Kumar
Mr Ashok

KENYA

Abdalla Rifai
Mohamed Mbarak
Mohamed Shamuti

Khadija Abdillah Mohammed
Abdul Rahman Zubeiri
Abdurazak Ali

Abdila Rifai
Said Mohamed
Ali Ahmad

Working in Kenya through the Kenya Society for the Protection and Care of Animals (KSPCA):

Dr Solomon Onyango
Alfred Shidula
John Maina
Wycliffe Gwatemba

John Akumonyo
Daniel Gitau
Amos Supeet
Zablon Jilo

George Agesa
Daniel Nzivo
Joseph Kiarie

ETHIOPIA

Professor Feseha Gebreab
Dr Hundera Sori
Amare Hundessa
Masho Tadesse

Dr Getachew Mulugeta
Rahel Woredework Belaineh
Yirga Gebremariam
Jermen Alemi

Dr Bojia Endebu
Alemayehu Fanta
Tsigu Shiferaw

Working on epidemiological study in Amhara and Tigray provinces, Ethiopia:

Keith Powell

Bekele Hailu

Dr Genene Regasa

MEXICO

Emeritus Professor Aline de Aluja
Dr Maria Elena Garcia
Dr Jaime Hernandez
Isabel Arreola

Dr David Montiel

Dr Alfredo Cabanas
Nelly Villalobos
Marco Sevilla

Dr Horacio Chavira

Dr Mariano Gil
Angel Carmona

EGYPT

Dr Mourad Ragheb

Hassan Thabet Hamoud

Said Tawab

SPAIN

José Rodrigues Gíl

Supporters who have attended Donkey Week for 10 years or more:

Top Row: Maureen Flenley, Lloyd Rogerson, Tony Wyman, Valerie Wyman, Jackie Bolton, David Bolton, Jayne Pearson, Janette Pearson, Jill Cook, David Cook, Barbara Dowdle, Gill Dowdle, Marjorie Flavell, Peter Broster, Lynne Anderson, Lorraine Morris, Bill Trinder, Jacqui Wells, Pam Crabb, Peter Thorne, Janet Jenkins, Brian Jenkins

Middle Row: William Scott, Lesley Shearman, Edna Rogerson, Mary Semark, Sylvia Horne, Margaret Mason, Olive Painting, Ron Wheeler, Chris Chesher, Mary Rudge, John Rudge, Rob Grigg, Marilyn Grigg, Sally May, Phil Hall, Penny Hall, Barbara Leppert, Melody Leroy, Ellen Shrimpton,

Bottom Row: Ian Stewart, Betty Stewart, Joyce Cadley, Joyce Friend, Margaret Bragg, Phil Wheeler, Judith Moore, Carmen Graham, Eric Nash, Dorothy Ward, Adrienne Nash, Dr Elisabeth Svendsen, Paul Svendsen, Phillip Rawling-Smith, Cathy Thompson, Jean Prutton, Ruby George, Grace Summers, Sarah Hall, Audrey Atherton, Barbara Sharman, Janet Thorne, Christine Quaddy, Eve Trinder

Not included in photograph: Barbara Abercrombie, Adam & Wendy Tinwell, John & Terri Jenkins

I N D E X